AGENDA

Testaments

Memorial

The angels keep

> The angels keep their ancient places;
> Turn but a stone, and start a wing!
>   Francis Thompson *(The Kingdom of God)*

(For the children killed in Manchester, May 22, 2017)

The angels keep their ancient places.
Turn but a stone, and start a wing.
See their stolen childhood faces,
an iPhone, a hairband covered in bling.

The angels hold them in new spaces,
dress them in clouds as they swing
from prayers, doing up their sneakers' laces,
each one a popstar now who sings.

The angels arrange three-legged races,
invite them to cart-wheel in a ring.
They will shower us with graces
if we turn but a stone and start a wing.

AGENDA

CONTENTS

FOREWORD **Andrew Moorhouse**		6
INTRODUCTION		8
TWO LONG POEMS		
John Fuller:	Blodeuwedd	11
Lynne Wycherley:	(from) *The Testimony of the Trees*	18
CENTENARY ESSAY		
Tony Roberts:	'All's misalliance': Robert Lowell in England	25
POEMS		
William Bedford:	The Moving Field	35
Rebecca Hurst:	The Early Medieval Balkans Holy Fool	36
Abegail Morley:	On keeping yourself whole and giving nothing away On not giving evidence	39
Matt Howard:	On the Tenacity of Life Small Tortoiseshell	41
Séan Street:	The River Test, Timsbury	44
Stuart Pickford:	Shingle Street	47
James Roberts:	The Scarecrow Makes Himself Border Crossing	48
David Seddon:	Headland Ships	50
Thomas Day:	Voiceprint	52

Aileen Paterson:	Slow Shutter	53
Craig Dobson:	The Reed Warbler's Tale Sightings	55
Omar Sabbagh	The More And More	56

REVIEWS

Adam Feinstein:	Then Come Back: The Lost Neruda Poems	58
Patricia McCarthy:	Pedestals	62
W S Milne:	Ad Terminus	78
Shanta Acharya:	Truth's 'superb surprise'	89
Byron Beynon:	Concord of Sound	94

POEMS

Robyn Rowland:	The habit of leaving Different ways with love	99
Jessica Mookherjee:	The Foreigner The River God's Daughter Becoming British	104
Jean Atkin:	Dialects of the Coppice Tremulant to swell	107
Mimi Khalvati:	The Brag The Void	109
Iain Britton:	Two poems from *The Primitives*	111
John Wheway:	Fruit	112
Laurence Wilson:	Protection	114
David Ball:	The Cemetery Going Down To the Sea At the Ballet	115
Jane Lovell:	Eclipse Milk Tapetum Lucidum	117
Rainer Maria Rilke:	The Carillon, Bruges translated by **Will Stone**	122
Will Stone:	The White Moor	123
Anne Lawrence Bradshaw:	Different Skies	124

THREE FIRST COLLECTIONS

Reviewed by **Josephine Balmer** and **Abegail Morley** 127

CHOSEN BROADSHEET POET

Laura Potts: Alma Mater 135
Swansea Son
Ernie
Holly

NOTES FOR BROADSHEET POETS 140
Clive James' 'Letter to a Young Poet',
compiled by Patricia McCarthy

BIOGRAPHIES 142

Front cover: Seod ('Little Gem') by Áine Ní Chíobháin courtesy of The Greenlane Gallery, Holyground, Dingle, Co. Kerry, Ireland www.greenlanegallery.com

Áine Ní Chíobháin was born in Cork City with family roots in Corca Dhuibhne. She has been living and working in Dingle since 2007. She has an Honours Degree from Crawford College of Art and Design, Cork City. Her artwork is found in many public and private collections. She is a recipient of numerous awards including bursary awards, project awards, and residency awards from Ealaín na Gaeltachta (Arts Council of Ireland & Údarás na Gaeltachta), Kerry County Council and Cork Film Centre.

Images in this issue in pen and ink by Sarah Longley

Born and raised in Belfast and now living in Scotland, **Sarah Longley** has exhibited in many locations including the Peppercanister Gallery (Dublin), Mullan Gallery (Belfast), the Fenderesky Gallery (Belfast), the Royal Scottish Academy, the Royal Hibernian Academy and the Royal Ulster Academy. Her recent work has been inspired by her new home in the West Highlands. She is very interested in the theme of motherhood and she depicts her own children within the garden or landscape.

Foreword

Editor's Note: we are delighted to have the pen and ink drawings of **Sarah Longley**, daughter of **Michael Longley** (whose new collection is reviewed on page 66) to separate each section in this issue. Two beautiful art books show the collaboration father and daughter have, as outlined below.

Andrew Moorhouse

John Updike said: 'A book is beautiful in its relation to the human eye, to the human hand, to the human brain and to the human spirit'. It is this quotation which inspired me to get involved in Fine Press publishing.

I'd collected Updike's books for a while, the trade editions, then the limited editions produced by independent publishers. Some of these publishers had their own presses printing the books. Others used specialist printers choosing letterpress hand-set type and sometimes incorporating commissioned images in response to the author's words. It was these editions that I'd liked best. One example is Updike's *In the Cemetery High Above Shillington*. The book presents Updike's long poem with wood engravings by Barry Moser.

I decided that, as a hobby away from my rather mundane nine to five job, I wanted to do something similar.

I'd also collected the work of Simon Armitage. Simon had just finished the Stanza Stones project, six poems on the theme of water carved into rocks on the Pennines. I got to know Simon and suggested that I might do something with the poems. Remarkably, as I had no experience in publishing, he said yes. I then just needed to figure out how to do it.

I was lucky to find a wonderful printer, John Grice, at the Evergreen Press, and John suggested Hilary Paynter would be an excellent choice to produce wood engravings. Guided by John, Hilary and Patrick Roe at the Fine Book Bindery, the 183 copies of my first publication, *In Memory of Water*, entered the world. I then had to find some customers. I contacted a small number of book dealers and tried to spread the word via social media and at Simon's poetry readings. It went quite well. The book is beautiful and buyers were very complimentary about the way that Simon's poetry and Hilary's engravings had been presented.

Simon then offered the opportunity to publish poems he'd written in response to stories from the First World War. My second publication, *Considering the Poppy*, with wood engravings by Chris Daunt, was published in October 2014 and sold out within five months. I was delighted, but conscious that I needed to add other poets to what grander publishers might call their 'stable'.

I'd read, and been intrigued by, a book, *Love, Poet, Carpenter*, in which authors wrote about Michael Longley. In addition, his collection *The Stairwell* had just been published and I'd recently studied some of Michael's Homeric poems on a Poetry School course. I travelled to the Winchester Poetry Festival to introduce myself to Michael who was immediately enthusiastic and, not too long afterwards, he gave me a dozen poems. Michael suggested that his daughter, Sarah Longley, should illustrate the book. Sarah provided twelve lovely pen and ink drawings. My publication would be called *Sea Asters*.

I talked to John Grice about the format of the book: the page sizes, the layout, the quality of the paper and print font to be used. I talked to Patrick Roe about the cloths to be used for the binding and what leather to use for the spine of the standard and deluxe editions and for the fully leather bound 'presentation' edition of the book. *Sea Asters* was another success.

I then approached Andrew Motion at an event, gave him a copy of *In Memory of Water* and soon after his Ted Hughes' Award winning *Coming Home* poems arrived in my inbox. Jane Lydbury provided seven stunning engravings for this book.

I've since published another Armitage edition, *Waymarkings,* and another with the Longleys, *The Dipper's Range*. I'm currently working on a book of Paul Muldoon's song lyrics to be illustrated by commissioned oil paintings by Paul Wright.

I believe that my six publications to date, utilising the considerable talents of excellent poets, printers, illustrators and book binders, have lived up to Updike's assertion about the beauty of the book.

Introduction by Patricia McCarthy

Welcome to this Testaments issue of *Agenda*.

A recent Poetry Magazine Fair – the first one of its kind to specialise in poetry journals – in Exmouth Market, London demonstrated the thriving nature, still, of poetry journals, despite the increasing prevalence of (often free) online journals, and poetry competitions on which money that could go to subscriptions is spent, the entrant probably looking for a quick, easy route to 'fame'. It used to have – and au fond still does have – as much kudos to be published in a journal such as *Agenda*, *PN Review* etc. as to win a competition – and poets need to be reminded of this. They also need to be reminded that in order for them to survive as poets, poetry magazines (and poetry publishers) need to enlist them as readers; and anyway to read a lot of poetry discriminately is surely as instructive and valuable a means to cultivating and expanding your own especial voice as attending an expensive workshop.

There have always been debates about the 'I' in poetry: the confessional 'I', the fictitious 'I' of the dramatic monologue, for example, and/or, most importantly surely the 'I' that can have a self but resists its too often attendant ego. This 'I' belongs to those few who are properly self-aware, rather than self-absorbed; who write not out of a sense of narcissism with its concurrent requisite for fame, but from a genuine wish to communicate, via craft, inspiration and musicality, what cannot usually be said in normal speech. This is the 'I' surely that expands beyond the personal to become a universal 'I' and in that sense anonymous, no matter what specific details attach to it. These different 'I's go in and out of fashion, except, I believe, for that universal 'I' that belongs to the more rarified species, the poète-savant, who follows Aristotle's well-known dictum: 'Know thyself'.

Poets and readers should do well to remember, as the neuroscientist V S Ramachandran explains in his book *The Tell-Tale Brain*, about 150,000 years ago there was an explosive development in the human brain where, among other things, we gained the ability to examine our own thoughts, feelings and behaviours, as well as to see things from another's point of view. Not only did this transformation create the foundation for art, including poetry, spiritual practices and language, it came with a survival advantage for our ancestors, who had to work together in order to survive.

In the latest issue of *Poetry Ireland Review*, issue 121, edited now by Eavan Boland, gifted poet Theo Dorgan writes very honestly about his relationship, as a student and friend, with John Montague who died only recently. As a young poet, Dorgan refreshingly disdained position and status, clear on one point 'that the only specific against both destructive vanity and disappointment was a ruthless concentration on the poem, the poem itself and the poem only.' He chimed in with fellow-poet Thomas McCarthy's poem, 'Daedalus the Maker' which claimed that the artist's highest duty was 'to lay art anonymously at earth's altar'. This, to me, does not mean that the poem must not have an author; it needs that universal 'I' in order to be given away anonymously, and left there for readers to have a silent dialogue with it or to make of it what they will.

Agenda has never been a slave to fashion; in fact, it has always eschewed the ephemeral, fashionable poetry that is surely in vogue one day and out of vogue the next. This is where I feel *Agenda's* importance still lies: to strike out for a poetry that matters, that does help us all, as said above 'to work together in order to survive', a poetry that is not just decorative, not just after an easy chuckle, not just intellectually clever, arid and cold as a fish.

It would be interesting to hear readers' responses to the points raised above so perhaps you would like to send in letters for a new 'Letters Page', establishing important debates.

John Fuller

Blodeuwedd

i

Lleu Llaw Gyffes is my name and pride,
Son of Arianrhod, who gifted me
With everything that witchcraft could provide:

Speech of the creatures, power of prophecy,
The strength to carry granite in my hand,
And more—mysterious immortality.

For how can you kill me? How could it be planned?
She left these five conditions to be obeyed,
Five strange provisos if I'm to be unmanned.

Five paradoxes leave me unafraid:
I may not be killed either clothed or naked, nor
With any weapon that is lawfully made.

Neither riding nor walking, neither outdoors or
Indoors, and I may not die by day or night.
So, by these fates I live, and furthermore

I am a lion on this peopled height,
And though I'll never have a human bride,
I'll live forever in my golden light.

ii

The stone is without fault. It settles, and
It stays where it is put. It will not crack.
I built the village in a month by hand.

Filthy hovels where the smoke blows back,
A pair of grey eyes staring from a bed
And something slightly stirring in a sack.

I help them as I can. I keep them fed.
I help them with the gathering in of hay.
I help them laying out their many dead.

They worship me, and in return I may
Do what I will with them. And where I've stood
The ground is kissed and sacred. Every day,

Like the wise bird passing from wood to wood,
Silent of beak and wing, till the dawn pales,
I pass among them, knowing the stone is good.

The stone sees all consents and all betrayals,
All vows and treaties. Here on this hill I stand,
Before me all the sea, behind me Wales.

iii

I light a candle as a sign of peace.
The flame is steady, though below it melts
As the peace falters and the raids increase.

Barbarians in their stinking furs and pelts
Leap from their boats at anchor off the shore
And wade the waves with axes in their belts.

The hill repels them. Bodies by the score
Litter the slopes, and all the booty ours,
Another battle in an endless war.

Yet still the candle burns through the long hours.
I speak to its bright silence with my prayers
And I give thanks to it for all my powers.

Sometimes along the coast I can see flares
Which might be either warnings or thanksgiving.
Who knows? Our neighbours' policy is theirs.

They have their foes, and fate is unforgiving.
I think my guarded hill a masterpiece.
It is a tribute to the art of living.

iv

My mind is pure as air. I stoop to let
The water trickle through my fingers, fall
Away between the stones to pay its debt

To gravity, race through the wood with all
The eagerness of youth to be elsewhere,
To splash, to glitter, bubble, leap and sprawl.

The way it follows is its own affair.
It does not know that it will meet the sea.
It has no thought of what will happen there.

And the grey ocean in its anarchy
Swirls up against this hill and tears at it
Like a bound creature desperate to get free

Of chains, who knows that time is infinite
And is an enemy who gives no quarter.
O innocent streams, you willingly submit,

Each a free spirit, each a faithful daughter!
You tumble onwards, never to forget
Your destiny within the parent water.

v

What was the charm that Math and Gwydion spoke
To form a bride in fullness of her powers,
Wholly alive, that only just awoke?

A bride of mystery, a face of flowers,
Complete in everything, like a young colt
Whose birthing after several restless hours

Makes an unfolded entry with a jolt
On to the grass, a knock-kneed stagger to
Assert its height, a shooting of the bolt

That turns it into legs and speed, and who
Could think it had not been for ever there,
Finding the world around it, green and blue?

What charm to find such bride of earth for air?
What magic for my ecstasy? Ill-fated
Destiny that only two could share?

My life, my future, in a flash created
From flowers of broom and meadowsweet and oak,
The golden hair with earth's sweet savour mated?

vi

As though a curtain rose. The tips quiver.
It is the ordination of desire,
The soft ledges proud in the falls of a river

That lights the whole skin, spilling like a fire,
The length stretched out like some moist creature basking
Through the hot silence, idly, one entire

Long day. And light makes sculpted shadows asking
No questions of their shape and origin,
The quick heart knocking at this shared unmasking.

This is the nudity of monarchs in
Their great unrobing. It is like creation.
Or some significant debâcle, like sin.

Just for this moment there's no information
To tell me which. The blinding surface shows
No choice in its ambiguous notation.

Mind is eclipsed. The body only knows
Its lying texts too variant to deliver.
Spirit with light leaked out? The beast in repose?

vii

Each day she asks me questions, till the night
Comes, and then she asks again. We stand
At odds, like stubborn hill and circling kite

That knows what moves down there. I put my hand
On that proud skin and might be feeling leaves.
Some mischief that I do not understand

Gleams from her eyes. It is a spell she weaves.
Her hair lifts as if it took the air
In it. Her lips claim something she believes

And turns into a question, asking where
Could she have heard it, if not from me? And I,
Infatuated, smile and do not care

If secrets tumble from my mouth: for why
Should secrets not be whispered on my breath
To one that I desire, although I die?

The day is dwindling fast, my Blodeuwedd.
The candle's lit while there is still some light,
And you have means to bring about my death.

viii

The flame sits crisp upon the candle, where
The dusk contains it on all sides like hands
That shield it from the ever-restless air.

It sways and flickers, gutters and expands.
It wants to light me to outrageous deeds.
It wants to lead me into fairylands

Where princes gallop and even a fool succeeds
In asking the right question of the stone
When the foul vapour of the night recedes.

Yet here I am, unmated and alone,
A bearded root uptwisted for the knife,
Ready for death in fated form foreknown,

Wrapped in a net by my unfaithful wife,
With one foot on a cauldron, one on a goat
Outside the window, my immortal life

Now bloodied by a spear the blacksmith smote
When all the people were at Mass, in prayer.
The fates fulfilled! She has me by the throat!

ix

Gronw Pebyr, the forger of my grief.
Gronw Pebyr, the fault in fellowship.
Gronw Pebyr, the instinctive thief.

Gronw Pebyr, the lie upon the lip.
Gronw Pebyr, the customary charm.
Gronw Pebyr, the greed within the grip.

Gronw Pebyr, the hand upon the arm.
Gronw Pebyr, the wedding vows unsaid.
Gronw Pebyr, the fingers in the palm.

Gronw Pebyr, the lecher's stealthy tread.
Gronw Pebyr, the milky face of guilt.
Gronw Pebyr, the stainer of my bed.

Gronw Pebyr, the tearing of the quilt.
Gronw Pebyr, the cruelty of power.
Gronw Pebyr, the honour freely spilt.

Gronw Pebyr, the instinct to devour.
Gronw Pebyr, the desiccated leaf.
Gronw Pebyr, the spoiler of the flower.

x

I am the Lord of Dinas, now undone.
Between the distant mountains and the sea
My burnished body takes the western sun

On glittering feathers, wings that carry me
Higher than crests of pines, higher than men,
My human form now a mere memory.

I am the Lord of Dinas, denizen
Of cairns and clouds. I am an eagle now
And I may never be a man again.

I scan the ocean with an eagle's eye.
My mouth and beak curl with amused scorn
Of those who thought they could make me die,

The meddling uncle and the bride foresworn
And all whose envy seeks my overthrow.
I leave behind the limbs that I have worn.

And there is nothing more in life I owe,
Nothing to her, nothing to anyone.
The air, the sun, the light, is all I know.

Lynne Wycherley

(from) The Testimony of the Trees

In 2016, scientists in Germany uncovered relentless
damage in trees much exposed to phone-masts' pulsing
microwaves, even at two miles. It was reported that
'this constitutes a danger for trees worldwide'.

I am the tree on the skyline.
You alone
know my name.

I stand in prayer-reeds,
Paschal candles, fragrant.
Hold my flame.

I am Acer Rubrum, queen
of the reds,
leaves in flow

crimson to crimson, your
heart's 'now'.
Shall we dance?

As if a Gale

We are floss, we are frail, in the ever-wind,
stems, serifs, pared back,

laterals lost to sky-wolves
as if a gale has shorn us from one side

staves to silence,
lamé to air, slow-motion.

In digital storms we are fraying.

What finger picks at satin?
What shadow sits at the loom?

Leaves on the love-tree, fading.

Hesitant child, where are you?
Your eyes wide to stems, to wings.
Hózhó: 'walking in beauty'.

Who weighs the harm, silk-grams?
Comet assays: genetic strands.

Who weighs the heart?
Ma'at with her feather,
Thoth with his reed. All buried.

Note:
Hózhó – Navajo
Comet assays – test for DNA damage
Ma'at – a powerful ancient Egyptian Goddess

Amulet

She's just looked up –
a candid gaze, a shell-like face,

lunette. Her *Silent Spring*
an opal under fire: amulet.

Her then: our now,
how the roulette spins –

adverts! adverts! –
'set phasers to stun'

    click-rates – war-games –
    children in screens
    their neurones firing, firing

while the slow wonder
of a primrose waits

its silk word held to heaven.

    My inch of sky, fathomless
    my well, my vowel
    my peace.

A Prayer Across Time

*'Workers in a Swedish office block have been
implanted with microchips'*
>   The Times

Love, do not sleep: it is coming;
do not sleep: meet needle
with needle, heald-frame, leaf.

Where do you live? Rail-sped
as copses, brakes, rush by –
> *a train: the-shell-of-a-train*
> *a phone: the-shell-of-a-phone.*

Box in box, estrangement squared,
the apple's scented integer mislaid
> *calling at: 4G, 5G*
> *smoked-out cities.*

Where do you live: a data
contact lens? Third eyelid, bat-wing.
How grey the veil, how thin.
> *Oak, beech, our branches inked*
> *on alizarin. Michaelmas fire,*
> *a hare in flight, unseen.*

Where is your friend? Dizzy, spent:
he's fled the hornet-nest,
the lightning, DNA in
a jewel-pouch for safe-keeping.
> *Lost friends, lost names –*
> *prayers across time –*
> *birds of paradise*
> *in Faraday cages*
> *fled from the fleeing world.*

Note:
Faraday cages – microwave-blocking nets used by electro-sensitives

Electro-Faust

'*Man conquered the Black Death but he has created new problems: electromagnetic-field pollution*'
                               Professor Yuri Grigoriev

> *Cross-fade, digital noise*
> *0 1, 0 1: needle-eyes.*

Trace it: a branch in cobalt
where metal spores nudge stars:
strange crustaceans, drones.

No 'white zone' in future-sleet,
subtle, the lace of life
left bare.

> *Yukiko, 'snowdrop-child',*
> *where are you?*
> *Eden-dot, light's dew.*
> *Lending your wick, your dazzle.*

No 'white zone'. Electro-Faust
in space, on land,
micro-wands: antennae.
No 'white zone': will a genome
furl its ladder

leave love midair

Dante's light receding
in pale rungs?

Note:

metal spores – the 'space race' to launch 11,000+ internet satellites
'white zone' – free of RF/wireless pollution

'The Lullingstone Oaks'

'Nor must be forgot...the translucent amber'
                              Samuel Palmer, 1828

Indian ink, heft in the shine –
how the oaks take life
in his cinnamon eyes
'barky furrows... these lords of the forrest'

> *Far, how you ebbed from us,*
> *cold-beyond-cold. Kelvar,*
> reductio, *deserts of code.*

> Space-walkers, stumbling;
> driverless tractors, driverless cars,
> hung from the not-here, frying.

> If birds could laugh! could cry,
> jays – magpies – blue-jade.

Almost translucent, the light
winning through: *citrinatis*
on white gouache

> *Cinders, strays: how you return,*
> *as if our stillness moves you,*
> *heartwood soothes you*

as lanterns quicken –
seeds from his soul –
stooks; apples; *rubedo,* whole.

Note:
Kelvar – bullet-proof metal used for satellites

Tony Roberts

'All's misalliance': Robert Lowell in England

> Conscience incurable
> convinces me I am not writing my life;
> life never assures which part of ourself is life.
> Ours was never a book, though sparks of it
> spotted the page with superficial burns:
> the fiction I colored with first-hand evidence,
> letters and talk I marketed as fiction –
> but what is true or false tomorrow when surgeons
> let out the pus, and crowd the circus to see us
> disembowelled for our afterlife?
> ('Marriage')

'Yet why not say what happened?' Robert Lowell asked in 'Epilogue' and saying what happened had, by the end of Robert Lowell's glittering career, become synonymous with the premier American poet. In fact the idea had dogged him since his autobiographical work in *Life Studies* (1959), his great, game-changing collection. Lowell (1917-77) was always ambivalent about this. After castigating the fallen world in his early, richly rhetorical poetry, he had turned to public address and to autobiography as a lens for history. Yet he was always aware of the complexity of the idea of truth and keen to point out the craft behind autobiography. Without craft, poetry would be merely baffled self-expression. As he explained in a *Paris Review* interview of 1961, 'Your actual experience is a complete flux. I've invented facts and changed things... so there's a lot of artistry, I hope, in the poems ... the reader was to believe he was getting the *real* Robert Lowell.'

In England, in Lowell's last years, the poetry became more personal, closer even than in *Life Studies* to 'the *real* Robert Lowell', though at times the art suffered. Initially energised by a new love, a new country, Lowell became entangled in the events of his life and confounded by vacillation, ill health and the bipolar condition that had undermined him since his thirties. That he produced so much good work in revised versions of *Notebook* (1970), in *for Lizzie and Harriet* (1973), *History* (1973), in *The Dolphin* (1973) and *Day By Day* (1977) is a tribute to his tenacity, honesty and artistry.

After a number of years in the public eye in America, through Democratic politics and anti-war protests Lowell was in retreat. As he confessed to his lifelong friend Blair Clark in May 1970, England was a relief: 'Things seem rasped and low in America, and here I sigh gladly into the somewhat different air. I'm thankful to get away for a stretch.' Lowell had been offered a (non-teaching) Fellowship at All Soul's College, Oxford, for April 1970 and subsequently a two-year teaching post as Professor of English at Essex University at a salary of £4,000, which approximated to his Harvard income. For a man steeped in European history and literature, as well as a privileged New England tradition, the opportunity to spend time in England was a further incentive.

Within a week of his arrival at All Souls, Lowell's life turned upside down. Faber held a party in his honour. Among the guests was the aspiring author and member of the Guinness family, the thirty-eight year old Lady Caroline Blackwood, whom Lowell had met three years earlier in New York. This time they gelled. Lowell had had numerous affairs in his twenty-one year marriage with the writer Elizabeth Hardwick, though these had generally been associated with his manic periods. (To Hardwick he had earlier written, in 'Obit', the fine, chilling lines 'After loving you so much, can I forget / you for eternity, and have no other choice?') This new relationship was the exception. In a poem to Blackwood, he 'wondered who would see and date you next, / and grapple for the danger of your hand' ('Mermaid'). He also captured something of the renewed optimism she brought him in the opening poem to *The Dolphin*, 'Fishnet': 'Yet my heart rises, I know I've gladdened a lifetime / knotting, undoing a fishnet of tarred rope'.

After the Faber party the couple returned to her home in Redcliffe Square, Kensington, where Lowell effectively took up residence. In the following weeks they took trips to Ireland and the Lake District, while Hardwick waited anxiously for news of the accommodation Lowell was supposed to be finding so that she and their daughter, Harriet, could join him. What she heard from Lowell was, according to 'On the End of the Phone', only 'My sidestepping and obliquities'.

At the end of June, Hardwick learned of the affair and was understandably furious, particularly since she had given up her teaching post at Barnard College and Harriet had been removed from school. ('My utter contempt for both of you for the misery you have brought to two people who had never hurt you knows no bounds.') Perhaps under the pressure of events Lowell's behaviour became erratic; another manic attack was on the way. After an incident at All Souls and an escapade involving locking Blackwood in her Redcliffe Square home away from her girls, she decamped to Ireland while Lowell was hospitalized at Greenways Nursing Home, London. He described his early symptoms in 'Redcliffe Square' as an 'old infection': 'lowered good humor, then an ominous / rise of irritable enthusiasm'.

Hardwick flew to visit him, assuming that this was another of those manic Lowell infatuations which often expressed a desire for a new start, a symptom of his mental state. She worried over the rumours of his neglect at the hospital, tidied him up, determined finally that he was in safe and returned to New York, offering to be there for him if he needed her. Lowell wrote appreciatively to her of their time together, 'You couldn't have [been] more loyal and witty. I can't give you anything of equal value.' It was clear that the three were tangled in their relationships. Blackwood returned but was unwilling to house Lowell until he was perfectly well. As he put it in 'Runaway', 'At the sick times, our slashing, / drastic decisions made us runaways.' The episode was a warning to Lowell about her limited ability to handle him in illness, especially given her commitment to her girls, something that Hardwick had done loyally, valiantly and repeatedly for many years.

In October Lowell began teaching at the University of Essex. He had been looking forward to it, he told Hardwick, because 'teaching is so much easier and more dependable than writing, tho so much less'. He was, also, working on a new collection, the sonnets that were to become *The Dolphin*, documenting his problematic relationships and, controversially, using Hardwick's letters. Despite the order the book imposed, the real order of events was disastrously confused, as can be seen by the letters exchanged at the time. In October1970 Lowell wrote to Hardwick, 'Even if I returned for good, if that has meaning, almost all would be unsolved.' Although he credits their marriage as being 'both rib and spine for us these many years', he also writes of his 'useless, depressed will' and of his love for Caroline. Lowell's vacillation was chronic. He wrote to Adrienne Rich on the same day, the 21st, telling her it was 'Hard to tell what is right or even possible'. Clearly much as Lowell loved and respected his wife, he felt the marriage had foundered. He continued, 'I imagine I'll get divorced, and all may be well, but the loss will never go.'

At the beginning of November Lowell was writing to his friends Peter Taylor and then Mary McCarthy that he anticipated returning to Hardwick. Five days later he mooted the possibility of a return ('Maybe you could take me back, though I have done great harm.') Even this early in his relationship with Blackwood (still married to the father of her daughters, Israel Citkowitz), Lowell sensed the impossibility of his relationship with his new, younger partner: 'To go on seriously toward marriage with Caroline against the grain, the circumstances, our characters etc. is more than can be got away with. We don't think we can, and are in accord.' He further said (then retracted), 'I do find though that even for such a careless person as me one is cemented in habits beyond belief. I had to come to England to live with practically new wife to learn my whole being is repetition of things once done.'

Essex did not turn out to be the dream he had first imagined, either. He found the university architecturally dull, second rate and the students less motivated than his Harvard students, but his opinion fluctuated. To Hardwick he reported in November 'My classes are small and quiet, the Poetry Writing rather retarded after Harvard, a good one in Shakespeare'. Later, teaching *King Lear*, he reckoned his students 'mutely thumb through their texts. I got so weary, I hardly read the brief assignments I gave. I am hoping to live off my royalties and "papers".'

Crucial to everyone's well-being was the 'baffling vacillation'. It was to feature in his poem 'Doubt': 'From the dismay of my old world to the blank / new – water-torture of vacillation!' He had warned Hardwick in October that he did not think that he could return to her. He loved Caroline, 'but allow me this short space before I arrive in New York to wobble in my mind. I will be turning from the longest realest and most loved fragment of my life.' He visited at Christmas, staying with Blair Clark, to whom he confessed, 'I don't know yet what will happen, but I increasingly fear the blood I'll have to pay for what I have done, for being me.' The visit was calmer than he anticipated and his daughter a pleasure to be with. Yet the visit held nothing for Hardwick except the knowledge she was losing him. His new life, he confided to John Berryman, 'fills me with uncertainties that mount up terror.'

In terms of his poetry, the one significant gain was in the presence of Frank Bidart, a former student of Lowell's, who had helped him revise and expand his collection *Notebook 1967-68* into *Notebook* (1970). While in New York that Christmas Lowell had Bidart meet him and look over the ninety-odd sonnets he had so far produced for *The Dolphin*. Although dolphins were not part of the book's narrative at that time, they became associated with Blackwood in Lowell's mind (beautiful,'bigger-brained than man and much more peaceful and humorous', he explained to his daughter). They also were to feature in a manic episode when he bought several antique versions for Blackwood's country house, 'Milgate' (Maidstone), where they were to move in the summer and Lowell would imagine himself among the squirearchy.

In the new year he returned to London and moved in with Blackwood at 8 Redcliffe Square. Then in February his marital vacillation became irrelevant after the disclosure of Blackwood's pregnancy. It took some weeks for Lowell to inform Elizabeth Hardwick. He worried about losing his daughter, had to put off his plans for a New York visit, but felt himself reborn at the news. Poetry took him to Scandinavia and Holland for readings. Other distractions were offered, firstly by Jonathan Miller's production of his translation of *Prometheus Bound* and then a genealogical Orkneys adventure with Jonathan Raban, who would edit Lowell's *Selected Poems* in 1975. Robert Sheridan Lowell was born on September 27th.

The weekly trips to Essex were a drag on Lowell's spirits but *The Dolphin* was taking shape as a narrative of the end of one marriage and the beginning of another. Word reached Hardwick that what Lowell referred to as his 'rather grinding autobiography' might not augur well. In December Lowell wrote to Bidart again requesting his help, this time in reworking *Notebook* into what would become two books, one public, one personal (*History* and *For Lizzie and Harriet*). 'This all began,' Lowell wrote ominously, 'by trying to get around the mounting pressure on me not to publish *The Dolphin*. (For moral reasons.) And indeed, it must wait.' But it could not, because he was as compulsive about his desire to publish as he was to write. He ignored warnings by friends like Stanley Kunitz ('There are details which seem to me monstrously heartless') and Elizabeth Bishop about the use of Hardwick's letters in the forthcoming book. She famously warned him, in a letter of March 1972: 'One can use one's life as material – one does, anyway – but these letters – aren't you violating a trust? IF you were given permission – IF you hadn't changed them…etc. But *art just isn't worth that much*.'

Lowell might have given 'Lizzie' the best of the lines in these poems as he claimed; she is still the supplicant:

> You left two houses and two thousand books,
> a workbarn by the ocean, and two slaves
> to kneel and wait upon you hand and foot –
> tell us why in the name of Jesus.
>
> ('Hospital 11')

The irony is made clear in 'Records' where Hardwick sees him as 'doomed to know what I have known with you, / lying with someone fighting unreality'. What could he say? Lowell was now settled in England with a new love. While America continued a lure of sorts – he wished to return 'temporarily' – there were binding commitments here. In January 1972, Blackwood's six year old daughter was badly scalded. Then there were the little daily dramas of living and the attempt to civilise their baby son.

In October the Lowells flew to New York to finalise divorce proceedings and then on to Santo Domingo where he and Hardwick divorced (as did Blackwood and Citkowitz) and then Lowell and Blackwood married. The settlement with Hardwick soon began to seem punitive, 'a barracuda settlement', since he gave up most of his trust fund, their apartment in New

York and his cousin's home in Castine, Maine.

1973 promised more poetry (the Rotterdam Poetry Festival), more leisure (fishing in Westmorland) and Harriet's visit, but the year was dominated by the imminent publication of the three collections. *History* and *For Lizzie and Harriet* did little to mask the arrival of *The Dolphin* and the critical response ran from the favourable English to the insulting American. Most famously Adrienne Rich wrote in the *American Poetry Review*, 'this is bullshit eloquence, a poor excuse for a cruel and shallow book' describing it as 'one of the most vindictive and mean-spirited acts in the history of poetry'. Rich was clearly on Hardwick's side, at least. Marjorie Perloff's *New Republic* review in early July suggested that Harriet and her mother deserved their treatment. Whatever it was, the use of the letters was neither vindictive nor mean-spirited in intention. Lowell's latest biographer, Kay Redfield Jamison, denies a moral case was involved in his writing the book, 'only a human and artistic one' for which overwhelming precedent existed. It was an unfortunate consequence of being intimate with an autobiographical poet. As Lowell put it in the book's final poem, 'Dolphin':

> I have sat and listened to too many
> words of the collaborating muse,
> and plotted perhaps too freely with my life,
> not avoiding injury to others,
> not avoiding injury to myself –
> to ask compassion

The fury and the heartbreak passed and though Hardwick interrupted their relationship, she did not end it. Lowell had continued teaching at Essex in the spring but moved to Massachusetts in the autumn to teach again at Harvard before returning to 'Milgate' at the end of term. Some sort of balm if not vindication came in 1974 with the award of the Pulitzer Prize for *The Dolphin*. Lowell gave a reading tour of the American South in the spring, before again returning to 'Milgate', but in truth his relationship with Blackwood was being undermined by their health and life style. Even in *The Dolphin* we have a strong sense of the turmoil of love and its blindness:

> I watch a feverish huddle of shivering cows;
> you sit making a fishspine from a chestnut leaf.
> We are at our crossroads, we are astigmatic
> and stop uncomfortable, we are humanly low.
>
> ('Fall Weekend at Milgate')

Putting aside themes of birth and rebirth, Lowell had begun what was to be his last book, *Day by Day*, a collection concerned with premature aging, conscience and regret. He put a brave face on it in one letter, describing it as facing 'time and age without hysteria'. Yet, as the title suggests, last things were on his mind. There is the recurrent terror of the manic episodes ('Where you are going, Professor, / you won't need your Dante' – 'Visitors'). *Huic ergo parce, Deus* (Therefore spare him, O God) one poem ends. There is wry humour too, in poems to Jean Stafford and John Berryman. Lowell's poetic masters had now died: Roethke, Frost, William Carlos Williams, Eliot and Jarrell in the decade before, Pound and Berryman in 1972 and now his teacher John Crowe Ransom. As he put it in 'Our Afterlife 1':

> We are dangerously happy –
> our book-bled faces
> streak like red birds,
> dart unstably,
> ears cocked to catch
> the first shy whisper of deafness.
> This year killed
> Pound, Wilson, Auden…

What he said of one he might have said of all: they remained lying 'alive like a feather / on the top of the mind'. Lowell too was ailing, a heart condition as well as the bipolar disorder. 'The doctors come more thickly' he wrote in another poem from the collection. He was also made uncomfortable by the economic climate in Britain and began to wonder if the 'enormous problems and irreconcilables' it brought might not prompt their return to America, 'where I can earn, have friends, etc'. He suggested to Elizabeth Bishop in October that Blackwood was having a nervous breakdown. The pressure may have prompted his own visit to a heart-specialist that month and in Boston in February 1975, where he had gone for the spring term to Harvard. He was again unwell, mixing alcohol with the lithium that had held off the worst of the bipolar episodes. This was to be a year of manic behaviour, with spells in Greenways Hospital, Mount Sinai Roehampton and Greenways. In between he prepared his *Selected Poems* and then, with the aid of Bidart and editor Robert Giroux, began to collect his prose writings. He also managed a poetry festival at Kilkenny with Seamus Heaney and a little salmon fishing.

1976 began badly for Lowell. As he described it to Bishop in early March: 'I had a longish though not violently troubled stay in the hospital, and have been out a month – mildly depressed… Mildly is bad enough.

Though I can't make too much of it. I fear the frequency of these things, fear becoming something that must be categorized as a burden.' He was still considering a return to America with the family, but felt the difficulty of disturbed routines and houses. Years of abuse of alcohol and medicine were taking their toll. In 'To Frank Parker' he mused, 'What is won by surviving / if two glasses of red wine are poison?'

In April Lowell returned to New York City for a bicentennial production of his play, *The Old Glory* (his trilogy from Hawthorne and Melville) finding the performance a disappointment. The city also failed to please him, now he had become accustomed to rural living in England. Better was a visit from Elizabeth Hardwick, in England for a PEN conference. He felt the three of them were reconciled. Lowell's honours continued, as did his problems. He attended Aldeburgh Festival in June to hear Benjamin Britten's cantata for his version of *Phaedre*. It was followed in September by Blackwood's decision to sell 'Milgate' because of rising costs. They were to travel to Cambridge, Massachusetts, but Lowell was first hospitalized. Christmas was spent in Scotland before he returned to Harvard in January 1977, when he was hospitalized for congestive heart failure but went on to teach again.

In his absence Blackwood had moved to an apartment in a stately home in Castletown, Ireland. Lowell flew over for Easter but their relationship was by now in grave difficulty. He wrote a number of poignant letters to her on the subject, including one of April 14th, 1977 which began 'I don't know what to say, our problems have become so many-headed and insuperable. Nothing like the sunshine of the years we had together – when it shone, as so often – so blindingly.' Caroline and Ireland ('all so far from home and help') both depressed his spirits. He wrote a week later 'I love you, am more dazzled by you than anyone I've known, but can't I be your constant visitor?' Theirs was a relationship in which each by now exhausted the other:

> Will we always be
> one up, the other down,
> one hitting bottom, the other
> flying through the trees
> ('Seesaw')

At the end of the Harvard term Lowell moved back to Elizabeth Hardwick and 15 West 67th Street in New York, from where they made a ten-day visit to Moscow as part of an American delegation to the Union of Soviet Writers. In May he received the Gold Medal for Literature from the American Academy of Arts and Letters. Although Blackwood attended the ceremony, their relationship now was too fraught and Lowell spent the summer quietly in Castine, Maine, with Hardwick. Later he visited Ireland to see his wife and son. There his restlessness worried Blackwood, who was anyway wounded by his return to Hardwick. She left for London and Lowell curtailed his visit after a frightening night locked in the apartment alone. His free verse collection *Day by Day* had been published to better reviews, but his life was ending. He died of a heart attack in a New York taxi returning to Hardwick on September 12th, holding in his arms a portrait of Blackwood by her first husband, Lucien Freud, which he was to have had valued.

The ironies would mount no higher. England had been a highly emotional retreat for Lowell. In the end he could not endure it and had returned to his former, settled life in New England. Even where the man failed, however, the artist survived. *Day By Day* ends with the wonderful 'Epilogue', a meditation on life and art and on the urgent need for recognition of our messy, transient lives:

> All's misalliance.
> Yet why not say what happened?
> Pray for the grace of accuracy
> Vermeer gave to the sun's illumination
> stealing like the tide across a map
> to his girl solid with yearning.
> We are poor passing facts,
> warned by that to give
> each figure in the photograph
> his living name.

*

Reaers might be interested to note that **Grey Gowrie**, who knew Lowell well, wrote a very fine 'Memoir' to the man in *Agenda*'s U.S. issue, Vol 41 Nos 3–4.

See inside back cover for *Agenda*'s Robert Lowell Special issue, Vol 18 No 3, Autumn 1980.

William Bedford

The Moving Field

'Then all at once there ran out a horde of rats.'
Piers the Ploughman: Langland

You leant on the gate and talked of dowsing:
the poet's walk across hidden water,
the hand guiding what the heart seeks.
'Cedar's best,' you said, 'my way of thinking.'

I prefer looking where I know what I'll find.
Not maps, but known landscapes:
streams, copses, familiar valleys;
the astronomer's way with stars.

'But you can never tell with fields,'
you went on, nodding out of some memory.
You saw a field once, moving in sunlight,
like a river surging for the estuary.

'It was rats, travelling across country.
Thousands of them, in a swarm,
devouring a whole year's harvest.
Nobody could ever have predicted that,

though it got to be common, after the war.
You could do nothing. Just stand and watch.'
We do nothing, in a fen twilight.
Two strangers, talking about dowsing.

Rebecca Hurst

The Early Medieval Balkans

The old map confounds.
A finger tracing boundaries
mistakes borders for rivers and roads
a tea-stain for a pearly lake or estuary
and an ink-fleck for a walled town.
Always someone going somewhere
in a tremendous hurry: call them
Bulgars or Avars or Ostrogoths.
Listen for steppe-sure hooves
treading the silk road to dust.

Lost in the woods northwest of Cluj
the envoi, asleep in his saddle, dreams
of wrestling a bear. He sways in its arms
a rough-ready polka. And wakes to the tune
of east-wind scraping against conifers.
The letter, *null cipher*, ticks inside his satchel.
He's in love with a woman whose tongue
he does not speak. There are three sides to this love –
her, him, war – pacing out the miles between them.
Blood flows like water and

the river has not yet reached the sea.
A week later and the eastern sky
is black with smoke and crows.
In the musty, cluttered gatehouse
a middle-aged man struggles
to fasten the fibula
of a tarnished breast-plate.
The buckle won't bite down
on the leather strap. He thinks,
This fit perfectly the last time I tried it on.

Holy Fool

In my beggar's mind, for the first time,
ditches open, full of brassy water,
and I follow them away from myself,
both the blind man and his guide.
        Osip Mandelstam

Children follow me
along the village's single street.

They call me Fool
but do not throw stones
as at the Tartar beggar-woman
whose very look can curdle milk,
cause a healthy child to wither and die.

Sometime ago I vowed to touch no iron.
The cross around my neck is carved from wood.
I will not hold an axe or knife or hoe.
Cut nothing, kill nothing.
I bind my feet in birch bark and felt,
wear linen, a stinking sheepskin coat,
wind a braided belt of scarlet
and gold around my waist.

I do not sleep among people
but alone in the forest.
Speak soft as leaf-fall.
Shy away from the touch
of another human being.

At the crossroads I kneel
and bow my head to the earth
three times. Then walk across fields
through acres of blue flax, golden rye.

I share my black bread with finches,
crumbs from my upturned palms.
Beyond the village lie untrammelled
forests and boundless steppe.

Fierce winters, frosty nights
have nibbled away at me,
reddened my cheeks and fingertips
but also charged me
through with some fierce blue light.

I laugh and sing as I walk.
Reach down and pluck
from the snow
a dead branch.
In my hand it bursts
into newly-minted leaf.

I lose myself in the forest.
I find myself there –
blindman and his guide –
feeling out the narrow paths
made by deer and wolves.

I sing as I walk,
Lord, lord, have mercy upon me.

Abegail Morley

On keeping yourself whole and giving nothing away

As soon as the dimming happens and sun spins itself
behind houses, she goes to the front window,

hands on sill's lip, its glossy coat under each finger's pad
comforts something in her as if her twin slips his hand

in hers and their young knuckles touch again. She thinks,
remembers him cleaving bark, penknife daring sap,

whittling twigs to resemble people, arms akimbo
like they'd been shot. Later it's not this she recalls

as she pours wine into an already sullied glass, it's the man
down the street, black-maned, who liked to play

boy-soldiers, would hold her too tight, say he could sniff
out a girl at twenty paces, on a good night.

This is his good night, twisting her arm with two hands
as if wrenching a jar's stiff lid from glass.

On not giving evidence

I use his thumbprint tonight. His mouth's still burnt.
Sulphur does that, so they say. I use his prints
because what I'm doing is because of him.

If you shake a tree something will fall – an apple,
an unopened bud, sometimes the whole sky.
When my sky fell they couldn't prise my eyes open,

so shoved tubes down my throat, needles in my neck;
they couldn't find my clothes when I was able to go.
If they'd swabbed those too, his prints, and all his prints,

would be limitless like memory, starting in a dark
back alley, shouting at itself until it woke an echo
in its belly it just couldn't stop, so it gathered momentum,

transferred itself to the scream in someone else's throat.
I am that someone else and it swivels inside a new shape
as if blown to shore by a heavy gale or a lone fist.

Matt Howard

On the Tenacity of Life

They caught it just south of the Doldrums.
Even *Half-lung*, our asthmatic Snowboy,
subject of their usual fun,
joined all hands hauling the albatross down.

In the panic, The Snowboy seized on its back.
He folded both wings, cradled the body with one arm,
and with free hand, squeezed the flailing neck;
inched fingers to the apt part of its throat and strangled.

In the quiet moment following death
the boy found his voice. He told of the skin's value,
that from such a specimen each man could take good share –
collectors and naturalists would clamour when we made port.

As he bid, one fetched twine, bound the feet, wings and beak.
Another brought an old meat cloth to cover it
and another yet carried the corpse to the port snow trunk
to stow safely there, on the highest shelf.

For those next ten days I took pleasure to observe
how he was now joined in their laughter. *Young Ice-heart*
they called him; a small marvel, a man
given to new purpose. Our passage those days was calmer.

On the eleventh day the dead bird grunted.
At the sight of a lamp it snapped the binds
and one wing, floundered, half-frozen, then slumped
to the floor. Aghast, Half-Lung despatched it again;

he ruined the skin with stabs, the skull with his boot heel.
Two broken ribs and three teeth were then excised –
naturally the hands were moved to violence
in lieu of lost profit. He was not seen for some days.

Upon his return he displayed contrition,
offered trinkets to all: albatross
fashioned into charms, earrings, fish hooks;
crudely engraved bones of the pinions for pipe stems.

For the Captain's children he made a Sunday toy -
the bird's thorax as hull, ribs as keel,
breastbone formed the bowsprit; sealskin stretched
and fixed so that the ark would float.

The kindness given to me was a flute,
which on his effort to demonstrate usage
I took at once; his blue-lipped wheeze
and shrill notes were simply too distasteful.

Small Tortoiseshell

The fen's particular darkness on this part of the line,
with its long pull over culverts, black-mirroring
the carriage's glass. Every passenger is inside and out
when the bonfire, already well taken, out there
between the dozing couple six seats down,
glows over the distance of each brow
like a butterfly, a slow-burn flickering,
that now glances across the pinned reflection
of my own eyes.

And I'm put in mind of the late summer just gone,
the luck or judgement, three-quarter-inch clearance
of a chrysalis above the front door.
Then the afternoon I came home early
and out it flew; a small tortoiseshell;
wings already hardened.
   How its blue,
amber and black must soon up-fold
to lift itself, its cindered underside
into some gap, when the first frosts come, some shelter,
say the powdery, adjoining mortar joint
around the lip of our back porch's flashing.

Séan Street

The River Test, Timsbury

'I could spend the rest of my life doing nothing else but trying to paint water.'
Norman Thelwell: *Merseyside, 1923 – Hampshire, 2004*

    i

Mersey to Test
    reflecting
        a life.

Childhood saw them,
    remembered
        horses,

Liverpool drays,
    cotton stacked
        like sails,

the city's
    waterfront
        epic,

the strain and heft
    of hoof dug
        between

Grimshaw cobbles
    for purchase
        to move

the thing forward,
    the sinew,
        muscle

machine of it,
    momentum
        gaining

grace from effort
    like flowing
        water.

ii

It's not the thing itself
but the space around it –
the air it inhabits –
that it leaves when it goes.

I turned, for the first time
saw light reveal itself
where the horses had stood,
felt the movement of time

freed like an undammed stream,
rushing in to fill up
the hollow they left there.
A kind of quicksilver.

iii

Component parts
       in painted
              water,

grasping silence
       that passes,
              showing

how surrounding
       thin places
              are breached.

Like the footprints
       waterboat-
              men leave,

I didn't quite
       break the skin's
              surface,

but poised above
        opaque deeps
                saw there

the reflection
        transparent
                sky gives.

        iv

A minute intervention on time,
childhood's remembered Liverpool drays,
Mersey to Test reflecting a life
in the caught flight of flowing water.

It comes down to just another day
when the sun here will roar on its course
over this, only another place.
I did not even break the surface.

Stuart Pickford

Shingle Street

There are no seasons on Shingle Street.
Newspaper stops us peering in shacks
with glass floats hung out to dry on fences,
the gardens stacked with waves of shingle.

Shingle grinds pebbles. Who dropped
the hag stones to worry our fingers?
Who picks them up to thread the eyes
with seaweed for children's white necks?

Shingle cordons off what we don't know:
the sea burning, German voices
commanding the dark, dead soldiers
bundled in trucks. Old farmers swear

the truth of it as night from day.
Shingle hisses when stepped on, saps
our strength, fills in where we've been.
Is it for nothing that we reel around?

James Roberts

The Scarecrow Makes Himself

He shivers at the door.

The howl of dawn climbs
the other side of the mountain.
It has just made a stream and a cliff.

He pulls on a skin
that no longer fits.

Today he will find gouges,
carve himself in wood
arms outstretched, head back.

He will wind the auger, bore a hole
and slot himself into the ground.

Crows will lay green eggs
in his open mouth while his chin
sprouts a hart's tongue fern.

He will stand sentinel at the field edge,
telluric, silent except for the notes
gales spit through his mossed fingers.

Border Crossing

So easy to become a bird
look at the blades on your shoulders
they are the beginnings of wings.

Already the lights are a long way down
the shadows they cast entomological.
They skitter and are eaten.

Lights going out sulphurous
like words deleted from a screen
erasing even our names.

Don't be afraid of the sky's cold,
it holds our deepest colours.

By the time we reach Franz Josef Land
we will have grown thick layers of down
and strong beaks to pluck new griefs
from the ice.

David Seddon

Headland

Here on the street
a gale rips
through the yards;

the spars of a carport
jut from a house
in the mist,

its bay cowling
a man caught
in a funnel of rain.

The sound of horns
and idling engines
drifts in the air:

the chances of
safe passage to work
moderate to poor,

I tack through rooms
dredging for words –
the pitch to take

to tell the boss
what I can do at home;
then the sea starts...

Ships

Sisters from the same yard
part at knots,
a single note on their horns.

Coasters separated by currents
catch a swell,
lights obscured in the dark.

Trawlers destined for impact,
nuzzle the rope,
cleave each other apart.

Dredgers billowed by gale
keel over,
capsize and plunge.

Tubs laid up together,
mothballed,
buckled, bygone.

Hulks beached-up by breakers,
gutted,
passing the torch.

Thomas Day

Voiceprint

For Eric Griffiths

The master's dog? True, you had a bark –
bitchily untangling 'the tumorous bitch' –
but your words 'the poet…' had an edge
too dutiful to be pure burlesque –

as if they were a species in themselves.
Your lecture was electric, I wrote
two days later, the stresses evident,
the hieratic punctuated

by a spritely wit. What was
that gag about closet drama? Was there one
about the poet *manqué*? Even to know that one
has lost one's voice, you wrote,

is an effect of voice. Your voice is missed.

Aileen Paterson

Slow Shutter

i

She is sitting on a hard chair, taken out from the kitchen
on a warm summer's day. You are sideways on her lap,
one bare leg along the hem of her dress
that whispers, 'flower-power, mid-thigh, mid-seventies.'
Your other leg rests on hers, skin touching skin.

In your tartan shorts, you are a young prince after a playful day,
your long ribbed socks, rolled down and wrinkled,
filling the U-shaped gaps in your buckled shoes.

You are looking directly at the camera but your mother
is looking only at you, one hand holding your wrist,
the other wrapped around your waist.

Her dark bob contrasts your almost-white mop;
the colours of the pair of you are in the dog at your side,
his long tongue almost licking your shoe.

ii

She is lying, not sitting, and *you* are holding *her* wrist.
Her hair is still dark. Now yours is too.
She cannot talk, only listen, and you tell her our secret.
She pictures you sitting on that old chair in the garden
with a white-haired boy on your lap.
Before the sun rises, she slips away
knowing you are a daddy.

iii

The morning after she has been turned to ashes,
I lie on a hospital bed.
You are a raw shadow over my belly moon,
eclipsing the new life
pulsing softly inside me.

I do not turn to you and grin.
I just squeeze your hand
that little bit tighter.

iv

Now, your arms are around our son
and your dark hair contrasts his nearly-white mop.
He looks like the twin of the boy
in the frame beside him,
the boy who is sitting on his mother's lap,
looking directly at the camera,
just as you and our boy look directly at me –
my earth and my sun.

Craig Dobson

The Reed Warbler's Tale

I took it for bus-judder at first.
Next, a tic's mothwing flutter
across her still-young features.
Only when we stopped mid-bridge –
the traffic frozen both ways
above the river's easy flow –
and she had to lean on a stick
to look out at the road locked
over the water's nestled swell,
and her reflection shuddered
again though the window held
perfectly still, did that unwell
immanence finally *tap, tap, tap*
through my shell.

Sightings

Not mermaids. No.
Not otters, nor the backs of porpoise
or head of a seal.
Not a loose lobster pot float,
or bobbing, unbound plastic bottle.
Not polystyrene's floating corner,
nor flotsam, worn log, whale fluke.
Not humps of weed, storm-dislodged,
Not the wind upon the surface, pinching,
nor a wave's shoulder boldened
in the greying light.
Not the light itself, blackened
on the water's back in shadow.

No. None of these. Something else.
Something I don't know.

Omar Sabbagh

The More And More...

For Faten

I imagine rock-climbing, slimming snowy caps –
The air is thin there. It's dragged across rocky, unknown maps
Where the muscles tighten, decking and decking their flesh,
And the juices are red there, redder, beyond redress...

Then I think of a deep lagoon, where famous men
Fish the sap of their souls, the dear and juicy den
Where they are furtive blooms, becoming, as become,
Themselves at last, beneath the crystal-brine, a home,

Beneath the white and blue, beneath the blue...
And then I think of her, lipping her liquid truths
Onto mine; and I think of how a candle's
Lit, the wick: beckoning the rounding air as fuel...

There are four of us there, between the sheets,
Two of whom are bitten, two of whom are sleep.
There are four of us there, seconding the night –
Its dram of dire gambit, with its X-ray sights

Needled upon the me in her, the she in me,
Echoing the tropics of a graphic topography,
An unknown map becoming read and known,
The more and more we close and hone, warmly

                          uttering,
                          uttering

                                      home,
                                      and home.

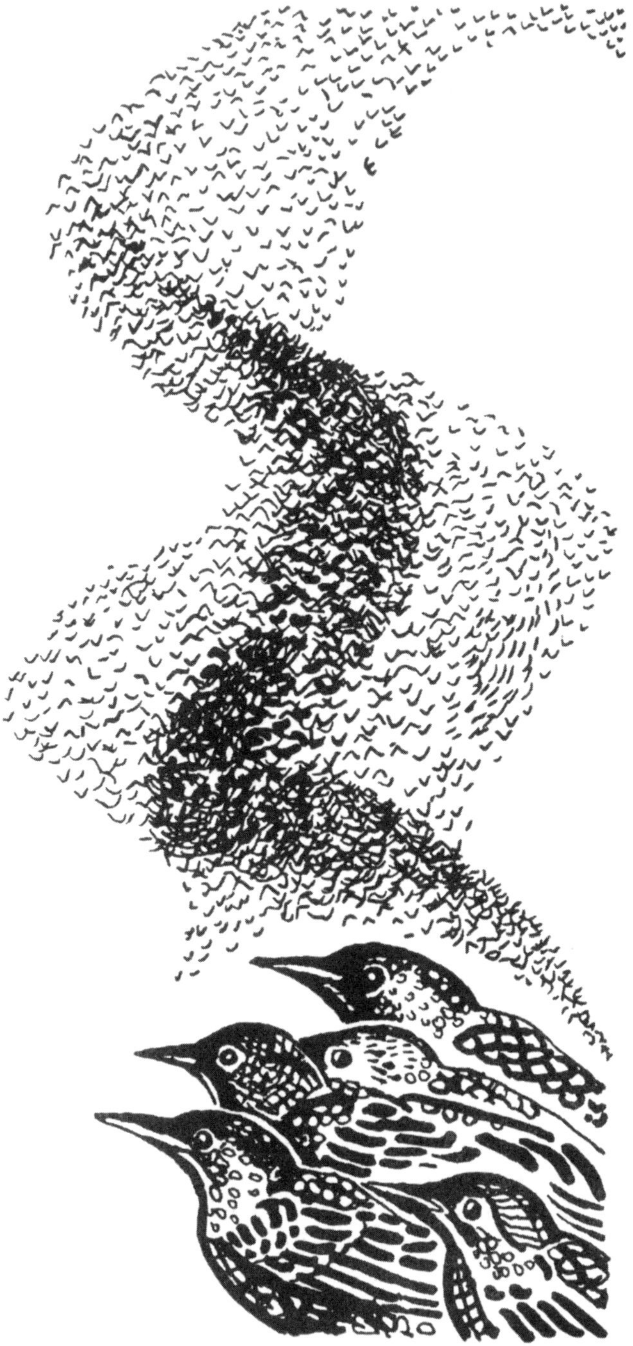

Adam Feinstein

Then Come Back: The Lost Neruda Poems (Bloodaxe Books, 2017)

Pablo Neruda, the great Chilean poet who won the Nobel Prize for Literature in 1971, used to say, perhaps only half in jest: 'One day, they'll even publish my socks.'

I cannot help wondering, therefore, how he would have responded after twenty-one unfinished poems of his – discovered in various drawers and boxes at the headquarters of the Pablo Neruda Foundation in the Chilean capital, Santiago, in 2011 – emerged in print. Seix Barral published them first in 2015 as *Tus pies toco en la sombra y otros poemas inéditos*. They then appeared in a bilingual edition as *The Lost Neruda*, with English translations by the American poet, Forrest Gander, published by Copper Canyon in the United States and now by Bloodaxe in the UK.

The first thing to say is that this Bloodaxe edition is extremely good-looking. It includes facsimiles of the original manuscripts of some of the poems – in Neruda's typical green handwriting – together with impressively informative notes at the back by the Neruda Foundation's Library and Archives Director, Darío Oses. As for the English translations, Gander's intimate connection to the emotional potency of these poems can be felt on every page. 'I have trouble reading them aloud without my voice cracking,' the translator himself says of the poems in his own introduction.

Variously scrawled on the back of a menu, the reverse of a music programme while aboard an Italian transatlantic liner, on napkins or scraps of paper, the poems date from the beginning of the 1950s to only months before Neruda's death in 1973 (just twelve days after Augusto Pinochet's military coup). They are all incomplete – presumably meaning that, by definition, Neruda himself was not yet ready for them to be published. Some even end in commas. There are instances where I believe Neruda would have gone back and made alterations, because a phrase sounded too clumsy. Two examples I would single out are 'cuanto canto' in Poem 2 or 'territorio terrible' in Poem 4.

And yet many of these poems are an utter delight, fizzing with an effervescent joy for life – and for that infectious passion alone, they are worth reading. Some have powerful echoes of the wonderful odes Neruda wrote in the 1950s in which, much like his great friend, Pablo Picasso, he made ordinary objects seem extraordinary. The appeal of those odes was that they were songs to specific objects which meant something to Neruda – a tomato, an onion or (in an exceptionally moving but little-known ode) a carob tree he had seen lying on its side, felled by a storm. In one of the most charming poems in *The Lost Neruda,* Poem 20, written much later than the odes (in 1973), Neruda bridles, in a glorious outburst of humorous agitation, at the despotism of the telephone,

> degrading myself to the point of yielding
> my superior ear (which I consecrated
> innocently to birds and music)
> to this everyday prostitution,
> affixing my ear to an enemy
> trying to take control of my being.

Yet this poem also has surprising echoes, for me at least, of one of Neruda's most famous poems, 'Walking Around', with its allusions to the burdens of bureaucracy, written as far back as 1934 in Buenos Aires, and also traces of Neruda's deliciously ironic 1958 collection, *Estravagario*, in which he frequently makes fun of his own social shyness and, in particular, of the witty poem, 'Poor Fellows', in which he gently protests about intrusions from prying eyes.

It is impossible to disentangle Neruda's life from his work and such glimpses of a temporal shift between different creative and personal periods make *The Lost Neruda* remarkably intriguing, especially for a biographer. Indeed, Poem 7, probably written in the 1950s, is Neruda's poignant and telling note to his younger self. It has resonances, as Oses correctly points out, of Rilke's *Letters to a Young Poet*. (This is hardly a coincidence: in 1926, as a young man, Neruda had 're-translated' a section of Rilke's *Notebooks of Malte Laurids Brigge* from the French – he didn't read German.) Once again, Neruda's pricking of his own pomposity in Poem 7 recalls *Estravagario*. But Neruda's advice to his younger self also highlights the transformation of his own work in Spain in the 1930s. Thus, his appeal to

>   dirty your hands
> with burnt oil,
> with smoke
> from the cauldron,
> wash yourself,
> put on your new suit

reflects his celebrated call, back in 1935, for 'impure' poetry and for an attachment to the grime of the quotidian. A year later, his life and work would undergo a much more dramatic metamorphosis from inward-looking anguish to outward-looking social and political commitment following the murder of his close friend and fellow poet, Federico García Lorca, by Franco's fascists in August 1936. Neruda described this process in one of his finest poems, 'Explico algunas cosas' ('Let Me Explain a Few Things') from *Spain in My Heart* (1937).

Poem 12 reminded me of Neruda's lovely 'The Poet', from his earlier (1950) epic collection, *Canto General*, much of which book he wrote while in hiding within Chile from the authorities in 1948-1949 – an extraordinary year captured in Pablo Larraín's recent film, *Neruda*. In 'The Poet', he recalled his youth marked by 'the deafest waters of envy / the hostile inhumanity of masks and other beings.' Here, in Poem 12, he refers more specifically to the political turmoil and police brutality he had witnessed as a student in Santiago in the 1920s. Oses believes this poem must have been intended to be included in Neruda's five-part autobiographical collection, *Memorial de Isla Negra* (Isla Negra Notebook), published in 1964 to mark his sixtieth birthday. How I wish I could have asked Neruda why he decided to leave it out!

Some of the poems in *The Lost Neruda* are (of course) love poems – either dedicated to his third wife, Matilde Urrutia, or to nature – or sometimes to both. (One of the great paradoxes of Neruda's life was that his train-driver father, José del Carmen, who was so fervently opposed to his son becoming a poet, unwittingly fuelled his verse with images by driving the young boy through the forests of southern Chile.) Poem 2, one such touching love poem to Matilde, written in 1956, contains many striking images, not only of the natural world but most notably (a point that no other critic has mentioned, as far as I know) *'el sol de una moneda'* ('the glint of a coin'), precisely the image he used more than three decades earlier in Poem 10 of his celebrated *Twenty Love Poems and a Song of Despair*. (That book, first published in 1924, went on to sell a million copies by 1961 and two million by 1971.) At the same time, Neruda's choice of a word like 'corollas' in this Poem 2 also presages the gorgeously lyrical last section of *Estravagario*, 'Autumn Testament,' also dedicated to Matilde.

Poems 15 and 16 are two further 'hymns' to Chile's natural beauty written in the final years he shared in Santiago with his second wife, Delia del Carril – the immensely cultured Argentinian painter who had played such a prominent role in Neruda's becoming a Communist, as well as acting as one of his most astute literary critics. When he showed Delia his manuscripts, she would write very perceptive comments in the margins, especially drawing his attention to his over-use of the word *'raíces'* (roots). By now, however, he was already juggling his life between Delia and Matilde. He separated definitively from Delia in 1955 and married Matilde in 1966. (Significantly, Matilde was the only Chilean of Neruda's three wives and, as he found his way more profoundly back to his roots through his love for Matilde, he chose to use the word *'raíces'* even more frequently in his poetry from then on!)

Poem 16 begins beautifully, almost elegiacally:

> Spring Day
> a long Chilean day
> a long lizard
> lazing
> on the amphitheatre of snow
> facing the navy blue.

Other poems are more sombre. Invisible enemies lurk within, shadows of Neruda's literary squabbles with envious rivals, Some of these allusions, as in the reference to the 'empty vanities' in Poem 9, are reminiscent of the 'Oda a la envidia' (Ode to Envy) from the *Elementary Odes* or 'El gran mantel' ('The Great Tablecloth') from *Estravagario*. But the overall spirit of *The Lost Neruda* is life-enhancing, even lusty.

Just occasionally, I found moments which jarred in Gander's versions. He elects to translate *'batalla'* as 'struggle' in Poem 2. I much prefer 'battle'. The reason is this: Neruda often employed a military lexicon in his love poems to Matilde – most evidently in *Los versos del capitán (The Captain's Verses)*, the collection first published anonymously in Naples in 1952. By now, Neruda was a member of the Chilean Communist Party and he saw no clear dividing line between his love poetry and his political poetry. In Poem 7, Gander translates *'la fecunda frescura'* as 'that tannic tang'. I entirely understand Gander's desire to retain the alliteration of the original Spanish. For me, however, the English version deviates too dramatically from both the meaning and the tone of the Spanish. The literal translation is 'the fruitful freshness' – which I am in no way advocating as an acceptable alternative! But 'tannic' suggests a bitterness which is absent from the original.

However, these are very minor quibbles. In general, Gander's versions are admirable in their reverence for the musicality and tenderness of Neruda's language and for the poet's ebullient, earthy and playful enjoyment of the world around him.

Patricia McCarthy

Pedestals

Alice Oswald: *Falling Awake* (Cape Poetry, 2016)
John Burnside: *Still Life with Feeding Snake* (Cape Poetry, 2017)
Michael Longley: *Angel Hill* (Cape Poetry, 2017)
Jorie Graham: *Fast* (Carcanet, 2017)
Emily Berry: *Stranger, Baby* (Faber, 2017)
Sinead Morrissey: *On Balance* (Carcanet, 2017)

It is presumed that poets seek fame. This is usually acquired nowadays by the poet gaining a glitter of major prizes, by the poet giving multitudinous readings at festivals and elsewhere, by the poet having good contacts, and by the poet being the main PR person for him/herself.

There are a few quiet, supremely gifted neglected poets always; and *Agenda* has taken on the role of championing these, for example Michael Longley (see Requiem issue of *Agenda*), Peter Dale, and Peter McDonald, to name just three.

Whether deservedly or not, some poets, via some of the above means, are put on pedestals, and once they are on pedestals, few dare criticise them.

Alice Oswald springs to mind. Alice rose to 'fame' with her accessible and very likeable coffee-table book on the River Dart. *Flowers and Weeds* was equally gentle. *In Memoriam* showed her tackling a classical work in a contemporary way to mixed reviews. Alice has her fans, no doubt gives many people real pleasure through her poetry, and she gives consummate performances reading her poems. Check her out on Youtube if you haven't heard her read.

Her new collection, *Falling Awake* might best be called *Falling Asleep*, if this does not sound too cruel. It is, after all, a very risky title given that her predictable and constant use of the same type of repetition, the constant use of personification like a little trick, and her childish conversational syntax all encourage the nodding-off. Yes, she is minimalist, but most of the poems are smug, tepid affectations; they certainly do not, as the dust jacket blurb claims, 'coalesce into poems of simple, stunning beauty'. Rather they are boring, pretentious poems, striving to offer vignettes of a rural life in England, but they do not succeed. If faint influences can be teased out, one could be the conversational part of T S Eliot's 'The Waste Land,' or the plays and novels of Beckett, Joyce but these influences are almost imperceptible and she does not seem to have learnt from those masters.

Yes, you could say the collection is musical and delicate, most often in a secret little coy voice; there are some strikingly original images, for example ' a rotted swan/ is hurrying away from the plane-crash of her wings' and 'it is so cold/ the bells like iron angels/ hung from one note/ keep ringing and ringing.' Or the perhaps childish but effective 'the woodlice at work in hard hats/ taking their trolleys up and down', the dew that fastens delicately 'the unknown to the known/ with a liquid cufflink'. However, only too often her images are obvious, even overdone, certainly not on a par with Ted Hughes as is claimed in one of the blurbs. For example the badger who works with 'the living shovel of himself' sees 'his own corpse falling like a suitcase/ towards him'; 'with the grin like an opened zip' and so on.

The repetition is the same throughout, used ad nauseam in a seemingly facile, twee way, with lots of spaces between chunks and lines that become an affectation. In the sequence, 'Village', for example she tries to use the ordinary vernacular of the working man whom she actually turns into a clodhopper, and keeps up the refrain 'say what you like' (used at least six times), accompanied by twice 'not many of us left'. The lack of punctuation presumably illustrates these village people's lack of education, or is meant to, but in fact it comes across as pretentious and arrogant, and at the last 'say what you like', you, the reader, want to shout 'But we don't want to say anything!'. She repeats this trite device in other poems not worth quoting.

Sadly there are too many quotes to pick out that can apply to her own stunted talent: from the long poem about the dawn, 'Tithonus', 'she never quite completes her sentence' but is 'always almost' is not meant to apply to her, the poet, but in fact it does. A little further on, 'the shining stuff' is 'just a cloth' heard 'in the grass' 'a bit like/ sound being reduced to sand'. I am afraid that is the impression this collection leaves this reader: not, as Jeanette Winterson claims ''making a new kind of poetry' with Oswald 'in the front rank of writers' – but, simply, sound reduced to sand.

John Burnside is a totally different matter. He deserves his pedestal; in fact a bigger pedestal than he has. His new collection, also from Cape Poetry, *Still Life with Feeding Snake,* has all the hallmarks which make Burnside a poet of real stature, each poem seeming to be exhaled in one steady breath, naturally, fluently, with no ornament, unforced.

In this collection, like his other books, bathed very often in snow, and dotted with epiphanies, Burnside harks back frequently to his childhood memories – 'are these our days of heaven in the end?/ These days when the world is mostly/ guessed at'... – linked to family and religion; in fact, the whole book seems threaded with biblical references, with titles like 'Annunciation', 'Confiteor', and the residue of his Catholic upbringing – phrases from the Church Latin – are inserted like 'in saecula, saeculorum', and 'that starched white on my tongue', when he had 'disappeared' at his First Communion. In this finely achieved poem, 'Memories of a Non-Existent Childhood', he articulates what many extra-sensitive children feel: 'someone on the far side, just like me/ but different/, his name a crude/ translation of my own, his body//darker. Sooner or later, I knew/ we would be exchanged'. Yet even when his childhood memories are graphic, there is always something interestingly askew and the poem often goes off on its own in an unexpected way at the end. For example in 'Sirens' he pictures his mother actually starting to give birth to him 'on the last day of winter' seeing a fox in a specific place: 'crossing a lawn/ at the edge of Dunfermline town', yet she notices 'the new fur// tawny and fine as silk when it turned/ to glance at the flashing lights alone in the world/ it was made for'. And then the poem takes its own particular turn and focuses on a successful, wealthy man returning home to his wife and daughters with presents. Their life is one of privilege, with holidays: 'He paints, his wife takes photographs./ Nothing can touch this happy-ever-after'. Here maybe Burnside is tongue in cheek and reminds of Larkin, the bourgeois ideal of a cosy, materialistic 'happiness' the best we can achieve. 'Sirens' demonstrates vividly the impact on the young boy he was – of watching the death of a young man who has come off his pride and joy, his motorcycle, after visiting his girlfriend. Burnside shows the shock and bewilderment he experienced at this time: 'Slowly, it seemed,/ he faded, like a stain,/ and I didn't know what to do'. His surroundings become almost surreal: 'our home woods/ empty and suddenly distant'. The contrast between the adult reaction (for example his mother sums up the casualty as 'just a boy') and Burnside as a young boy's is marked and reminds of Heaney's poem 'Mid-term Break' which again shows the difference in reactions to sudden death between a child and adults. Here, in contrast to his mother, the boy Burnside 'thought of him as a gift, his eyes dimming out/as I watched, at the quiet limit of my world,/ a kinship of sorts between us, right at the end,// when the ambulance came too late/ and I knew he was dead'.

His mother features in several other poems. In 'On Maternal Love and Filial Duty', the tenderness and closeness expressed for the mother matches Heaney's sonnets from 'Clearances' about peeling potatoes with his mother and folding the sheets. I would like to quote this poem in its entirety but will settle for picking out how his mother's 'secret love was for/ exotic flowers', yet on Mother's Day, he 'always brought her blue Forget-me-nots':

> ...how I am bound to her now, or she to me,
> I cannot say,
> but what I had is what we had
> together, all
> the pretty artefacts
>
> of sleep and superstition, fingerprints
> in glassware, animal
> horizons lit with frost, the cold
> exemplum
> in each blueprint of the heart.

Another equally remarkable tender poem about his mother is 'Mother as Script and Ideal'. Again the whole poem merits quoting – for ...'always, she is there,/ in lanternglow,/ a light that makes this world believable'. Burnside thinks back to the cold, dark house he was brought up in 'where someone, not myself,// goes missing/ while I lie down in the warm/ and wait for her to come',

>   her hands
> a labyrinth of mint and cinnamon, her book
>
> the only book we have, the pages
> thumbstained now, with daisychain and lilac,
> and such detail in the pictures, I could find
>
> The Snow Queen, or The Lady of the Lake
> so easily, is seems we must be kin.

In the extraordinary tour-de-force of the long poem well worth discovering at the end of this collection, with the refrain threaded throughout: '*The houses I had, they took away from me*' (Alice Oswald should learn from this poem how, exactly, to use a repeated refrain successfully to unify and stress in a poem), Burnside summarises and universalises the concept of mother: 'the light/ that makes us think of everything/ as Mother'.

This long poem, for me, is the summation of this book. The influence of Eliot's *Four Quartets* is quite apparent – all is an odyssey, with accurate and delicate interwoven images that evolve and develop, with properly musical use (unlike Oswald) of repetition.

As in his earlier collections, he is always in touch with the numinous and the hereafter, conscious of the immanence of the souls of the departed:

'Above us, souls are wandering in space;/ we know them all by name' and 'death lives like a long lost/ cousin, spinsterish// and hungry'. He always questions our meaning here.

Perhaps, in this book, there are more slightly prosaic passages than usual, but, in general there is no falling off (falling awake???). Far from it. The poet is assured and tackles big philosophical themes. The poems accrue and broaden out to include artists, fairy tales and myths, age, history, always with that enlightening touch. I cannot praise Burnside enough. He has won the TS Eliot prize and the Forward Poetry Prize, yet where is he re the prestigious Griffin prize? Alice Oswald (surprisingly for some including me, deservedly for her fans) – is on the shortlist where, in my opinion, she shouldn't be. This man certainly deserves to claim it.

Michael Longley's new collection, *Angel Hill*, demonstrates him, as always, writing pure, wonderfully accomplished lyrics. He did actually win the Griffin prize last year with *The Stairwell*, and highly deserved the accolade, as a major poet of our time. He has also, just recently, been awarded the PEN Pinter Prize for his 'unflinching, unswerving poetry.' Here he writes almost a last (hopefully not) testament, concentrating on old age, and youth, being a grandfather, his close, long friendship with Heaney (he resurrects him with realistic details and personal memories), on poetry itself – poets in the past, dead poets, poets now.

In the poem 'The Poets' he defines poets beautifully as 'Moth-and-butterfly-wing decipherers, Counters of Connemara ponies and swans' – and being a poet. Love poems – fidelity to his wife, love for grandchildren, and family members show him writing a more personal collection, with fewer than usual classical references and inter-weavings. A poem that, for me, particularly stands out is 'Fifty Years'. Here he offers a tender eulogy to his wife, highlighting their long, faithful, supportive relationship and demonstrating how she has been (still is) his editor and aide to his poetry-writing, supplying him with names and words, slightly reminiscent of Dorothy with her brother Wordsworth. We feel the endurance in the years in the very first line: 'You have walked with me again and again/ Up the stony path the Carrigskeewaun'. The 'again and again' represents a ritualistic habit. The second verse starts off invoking her too:

> You have pointed out, like a snail's shell
> Or a curlew feather or mermaid's purse,
> The right word, silences and syllables
> Audible at the water's windy edge.

In the third, final verse the two have become 'We': 'For fifty years, man and wife, voices low,/ Counting oystercatchers and sanderlings'.

'Room to Rhyme', in memory of Seamus Heaney (we have already heard about himself and Heaney as naive young poets in the little vignette of a poem 'Bookshops', and then in the amusing 'Menu' when he eats with young Heaney, young Muldoon and young Mahon) is another particularly memorable poem that takes risks with the music of its first and last lines. The poem begins:

> I blew a kiss across the stage to you
> When we read our poems in Lisdoonvarna
> Two weeks before you died...

And Longley proceeds in each verse to recount the gutsy, very alive, even humorous adventures he and Heaney shared over the years. In one 'We peed against a fragment of stone wall'; in another 'we chanted/ Great War songs'. Another time when 'Smashed after *Room to Rhyme* in Cushendall' they signed their names 'in biro on Davy's shirt/ And launched it off the cliff into the wind'. The poem ends movingly:

> Awaken from your loamy single bed:
> Kiss me on the lips in Lisdoonvarna.

Unlike Alice Oswald, who uses repetition gratuitously and, almost, as in a cheap Music Hall, Longley uses it for properly emotive and meaningful effect.

Place names and names of birds and flowers have their magical music that the poet is obsessed with. Carrigskeewaun where Longley spends much time in the West of Ireland echoes throughout, as in his other collections, as a place where he is properly at home, in touch with nature and the elements. He doesn't often enlarge on, for example, the birds he names, but when he does, such as with 'Starlings', a poem addressed to his deceased twin brother, the result is startling. The starlings are 'Swaggering opportunists/ Unexpected on the shingle' who become 'a shape-/shifting bird-cloud/, shit-legs/ Sky-dancing. No collisions'... He movingly asks:

> Wherever you are, Peter,
> Can you spot on your radar
> Angels? They're starlings really,
> Heavenly riffraff flocking
> Before they flap down to roost.

And real people strut these pages (unlike Alice Oswald's near caricatures of, for example, the village inhabitants).

Many of the short poems in the first half of the book can seem like slight smatterings, but they are so delicately conjured that they accrue like pressed flowers threaded through with fresh ones into a posy. Maybe this is what Longley means, at the end of the collection, when he states: 'Poetry is shrinking almost to its bones'. If so, they are fine bones.

His war poems are particularly strong and lived-in, probably so convincingly because his own Woodbine-smoking father fought in the War. The 'treasures' kept by his mother preserve signs of his life: 'the soiled underwear' and 'the strap from his wrist-watch/ With dust and sweat beneath the buckle'. In the finely-executed sonnet, 'The Sonnets', the soldier-poet who was not even 'a regular shaver' takes with him, among other things, the sonnets of William Shakespeare. He is then saved by 'the leather-bound book/ Which stopped a bullet just short of his heart/ And shredded the life-saving poetry'. Longley uses delicate images, too, which underline the poignancy of war all the more keenly. For example, the snowdrops 'between headstones/ on Angel Hill' – green-/ hemmed frost-piercers, buttonhole/ or posy' – are 'wintry love-/ tokens' for those home from the trenches. And in the fragile poem, 'Dusty Bluebells', the bluebells become the symbol for a little boy of nine who was killed by a tracer bullet, presumably in The Troubles in 1969. The children in his school resume their games, relentlessly continuing life, as they have to, with the haunting little song: '*In and out go/ Dusty bluebells, Bangor boat's away*'.

In the poem 'Bird-watching' he almost writes his own epitaph. So fitting are the images of birds, where he wants his ashes 'wind-scattered',

> I wouldn't mind dying now, I think,
> Shutting at last my bird-watching eyes,
> A starling-whoosh in my inner ear.

To try to plough through Jorie Graham's new collection, *Fast* (Carcanet, 2017) her first for five years so the blurb tells us, which won the huge Pulitzer Prize for Poetry in the US, is a task indeed. In fact to open her book and close it, to try again and again, and close it either points to the inadequacies of the reader or to those of this highly-acclaimed poet.

It is far-reaching as it spans cyber life, 3D-printed 'life', and biologically, chemically and electronically modified life, as well as our human plight on earth, caught in our limited time. However, so much has to be trawled through that to read the collection from cover to cover is difficult.

Thick, long chunks of what seem more like prose – on *fast-forward*! –

cause the book's pages to be larger than most. These chunks consist mostly of gobbets of phrases, interrupted by dashes, and, most annoyingly, these dashes for no apparent reason (or is this reader blind?) turn into arrows every so often. These phrases accrue with little or no meaning, as if on the verge of saying something so that the reader can't help thinking: well get on with it. But this never happens. I keep thinking of the title of one of Seamus Heaney's poems: 'Whatever you say, say nothing' – perhaps this poet's aim. Repetition again, little catch phrases of it, as in Oswald, is used ad nauseam in an empty way. In fact, to read Graham, is to see where Alice Oswald gets her inspiration; it has to be said that Graham is more engaged, though, than Oswald, even if sense is at times hard to come by, whether this is deliberate or not. This of course begs the question: does poetry have to mean something?

We all know that some poems do communicate at some subliminal level without being, or having to be, understood. We all know, too, that the existentialists of the last century prided themselves in peering into the void without any crutches of religion – or meaning, for example, yet surviving. Beckett comes to mind, but he is a dramatist, with definite patterns, echoes, style, humour, and profundity as he questions our seemingly meaningless and futile existence here on earth.

It is tempting to think of the novelist's techniques, and the attempt by Graham to apply these to her 'poems'. There is nothing new in using stream of consciousness which was deployed particularly frequently in American poetry in the 1970s, 80s and so on with varying degrees of skill, often tiresomely lengthy. Those frequently disorganised mental ramblings page after page seem stretched here into jarring, jerky passages lacking proper syntax or punctuation, almost breathless. Is Graham trying to use 'sound' in a special way? If so, where is the music?

Why not go for preference to Joyce's *Ulysses* or *Finnegans Wake* which contain far more what I would call 'poetry' than the chunks printed here. Or Penelope Lively's novel, *Moon Tiger*, with its deft handling of indirect free discourse, its startling use of imagery and cadence; or Virginia Woolf's *Mrs Dalloway* which is a full-length poem in itself, with all its skilful transitions, and repeated use of images which, as in T S Eliot's *Four Quartets*, evolve into further meaning whether direct or symbolic.

Of course, there are poems, passages and touches which are arresting and moving, such as those related to her attempts to come to terms with her parents dying, one by one. 'Reading to my Father' is a longish contemplation on mortality – 'The cease of. Cease of' – on what it actually means clinically to die:

Now I wait here. Feel *I can think*. Feel there are no minutes in you –

> Put my minutes on you, there, as hands – touch, press, feel
> the flying away

and on she goes, living up to the title of this collection, *Fast*: fast as her thoughts, not sparing the reader any details or ruminations, not allowing the reader to be, as T S Eliot said the kind that 'cannot bear very much reality'.

Her work is at its most effective when she focuses on the concrete, such as the list she gives of what her father loved. She is addressing him throughout the poem but it is as if he isn't really there:

> ... Here it is now the
> Silent summer – extinction – migration – the blue jewel-
> butterfly you loved, goodbye, the red kite, the dunnock, the
> crested tit, the cross-
> billed spotless starling (near the top of the list) – smoky gopher
> – spud-
> wasp – the named storms, extinct fonts, ingots, blindmole-made-
> tunnels – oh your century, there in you, how it goes out

The last line here is even reminiscent of Rilke. But these moments are rare. The father theme continues in 'The Medium' which does have an interesting focus – again there are graphic details of the father's agonising death and then he speaks from beyond the grave with his new perspective: 'The time for wisdom is past'. He says the mother must let go of her stories which are 'an impediment', while the speaker's (presumably the poet's) stories 'are all string and/ knot', they catch you up'.

Indeed, the stories Graham gives us in these poems are 'all string and/ knot; they need unpicking and undoing, they 'catch' us up with their garbles that are never quite garbles such as 'Dementia' which, to me, despite Graham's play with language, fails to capture the essence of this sorry state.

'Incarnation' is all about shape, again with interesting touches, in particular a passage on what it means to be a child, linking to the childhood theme in those of the other poets under consideration, here with a hint of social criticism:

> ... I was a child – my shape
> seemed a brushstroke – a thing about to be said out of
> respect for something or someone who had to arrive soon
> because we had built a system based on waiting and every
> thing – love respect fear – was based on waiting –
> so then you would be given your shape – and so

be honoured – there was a racket but that was childhood –
everyone was screaming all the time but that was words.

'From Inside the MRI' offers another original perspective, it has to be said. Somehow, amidst the panic of the patient in this claustrophobic tunnel, and the noise of the machine, a cherry tree, a classroom scene, and troubles of the world are brought in as the mind seems to play tricks. Even a screaming refugee appears running towards a chopper 'which will not land'. The lyrical bird at the end that sings signifies that time is up and the patient free to go.

The final poem, 'Mother's Hands Drawing Me' is successful in taking us through her terrified mother slowly dying, losing her mind, panicking yet drawing her daughter who urges: 'Draw it./The *me* who is not here. Who is the/ ghost in this room? What am I that/ is now drawn?' And the mother proceeds to rip up the drawing of her daughter, piece by piece as if dismembering her. The speaker movingly utters: 'I want this not to be/ my writing of it'.

Graham says in one poem: 'One must/keep trying/to make/ the unsaid said'. I am not sure she achieves this.

Emily Berry is a young poet and the new editor of *Poetry Review*. Her new collection, *Stranger, Baby,* follows on from her debut first collection, *Dear Boy*, which put her on a pedestal by winning the Forward Prize for the Best First Collection, 2013. Although it is possible to detect in her work influence from Jorie Graham and Alice Oswald – broken-up syntax, no punctuation, spread-out lines, use of repetition, she does reprieve herself by daring to journey through a distorted world in which she is intricately and heart-rendingly involved. In these poems she digs deeply, as in her first volume, embracing mourning, loss, pain, fear, recrimination, and, at times, exhilaration. The ground the poems tread is a dangerous one, where the self can disintegrate, or turn into another 'self' that is addressed in the poem 'The End':

> I wish you would put some kind of distortion into your voice
>   I tell her
>
> So people don't know it's me.

Here is evidence of the kind of depersonalisation caused by trauma or by being very disturbed. Her 'shame' is solidified into something that 'got hot, throbbed, wept, attracted fragments with / which it eventually glittered'. Quite often, as in 'Aqua' and 'New Project' no punctuation is used, demonstrating Berry's own bewilderment as her mother wears 'someone else's/ ghost': 'I was led totally/strung out every/ nerve onboard' – and it has to be said that this is the overall impression this collection leaves on the reader. It can seem, in many ways, like one long, high-pitched, at times fragmented, howl, reminiscent of Sylvia Plath.

The sea, often seen as symbolising our subconscious, is an important elemental image throughout. It can be both positive and negative, for example in the very first poem 'The Anchor', it can be a source of encouragement and something to emulate:

> Live your wish. Love your wish, said the sea.
> I wanted to be like the shells on the beach, rubbed smooth and
>   cracked open

Or it can destroy efforts at language:

> I shouted some words but they were lost when the waves crashed.

Then, in 'Picnic': 'Watching the sea is like watching something in pieces/ continually striving to be whole'. This is exactly what Berry strives for in this cathartic, psychoanalytical sequence, probably never achieving it: to be whole as she meditates on death, the loss of her mother, of the self, and on language itself or its failure to articulate what cannot be said. In 'Picnic' she finds relief in writing a poem, but even here there is something off-kilter:

> I like it when I am writing a poem and I know that I am feeling
>   something
> To be poised and to invite contact
> Or to appear to invite contact

Yet towards the end of the poem, she shows revulsion towards language: 'Stop. Language is crawling all over me'. It doesn't take much to guess correctly that Freud will be invoked – as he is, in four poems. In 'Freud's Loss' the language verges on the lyrical, even though Berry apologises for 'writing about such sad things'. The little carriage contains a mother and child:

> There is a kind of holy Sunday stillness over everything
> Huge mountains, some overgrown, some bare in strange formation
> You must imagine it like this:
> A two and a half journey through the most desolate lagoons

> A magnificent river
> Vaults, waterfalls, stalactites

She ends the poem by stating how 'to mourn' is 'permissible', but 'The rest – you will know what I mean – is silence', in other words where language cannot go. In 'Girl on a Liner' where she asks: 'Does crying age one? If so, I suppose I've become very old' we still feel that the actual writing of poetry helps her to survive:

> I watch the water pour out of my eyes; there was a feeling
> but I wrote it down and it ceased to be a feeling,
> became art

Though bereft, abandoned, and alone, at times full of anger and blame, she rejects others as in 'Drunken Bellarmine' when, full of self-hatred, she defines herself as 'a shitting, leaking, bloody clump of cells', as she cries out 'DON'T LOVE ME: I am guilty / fatalistic and sticky around the mouth like a baby'.

This 'baby' image is linked to her invocation of childhood (as in John Burnside's new collection) though here, because of her mother's death, she is almost forcibly reduced to being a little girl again, and uses childhood language authentically as a means of coming to terms. This differs from Alice Oswald's twee use of simplistic language for external effect.

For example, in the moving poem 'Winter' describing her mother as 'very very sad', Berry uses simple childish language throughout yet learns 'a new kind of love' and how 'to pray' for her mother: '*A prayer for the dead alive inside the living*'. Again, in the long poem towards the end of the collection, 'Ghost Dance', the real little girl, presumably Berry herself, demonstrates the child's attempt to deal with the mother's death, striking a haunting elegiac tone:

> People you love can be removed from the world
> (They can remove themselves)
> They will be removed from the world
> Didn't anybody ever tell you that

She is in Burnside territory in her dealing with death, presences and the other side, and this proximity is even more apparent towards the end of the collection where, like Burnside, she emphasises the need for the safety of a home: 'I was in a room inside a room./ There I felt safe'. Her grand finale is a little akin to Burnside's. New perceptions are granted by her mother's death, and forgiveness granted all around:

You took me over and I cried the way a sea cries
I cried the way a sea cries when it has swallowed a river

And she concludes:

Why is it that I can no longer bear travelling?
Why is it that I keep trying, like a lost child to 'get home'?

In the final poem, this questionable home seems to be the trees' arms which are her mother's.

The mother/tree urges her to survive. Everything comes, healingly, a full circle as she speaks to the trees in their language 'which can't be transcribed' and they agreed to fulfil her plea: 'Be my mother'. As Berry stated earlier in a memorable line:

'The dead don't die. They look on and help'.

Sinead Morrissey is another poet who sits on quite a few pedestals. She won the National Poetry Competition amongst other prizes, and the judges who awarded her the T S Eliot Prize in 2013 praised her 'beautifully turned language', and this is the case in her new collection, *On Balance* (Carcanet, 2017). Wide in range both geographically, historically and thematically, the poems here are cleverly woven around some of the great feats of engineering to demonstrate the states of balance and imbalance that have shaped our history. In amongst these are poems tackling gender inequality, our inharmonious relationship with the natural world, and various figures, including the Northern Irish Lilian Bland, first woman to build and fly her own aeroplane in 1910, Marconi who believed that the radio he invented in 1898 could pick up the voices of the dead, Napoleon's horse, Marengo, and events such as the launch of the Titanic in Belfast Lough, the expedition to Greenland (in which Morrissey shows her gift for dramatic monologues).

This collection, which contrasts being thrown off-balance with equilibrium, is itself a balancing act. It is a real tour-de-force, as many-angled as *Parallax* (her T S Eliot prize-winning collection) as evidenced in the poem 'Meteor shower' where the poet says 'we angle ourselves/ at a slant'. This she continues to do, but pushes herself further, demonstrating an even greater virtuosity with different forms and themes. Her rich, original language is so 'beautifully turned' throughout, with such accurate, sometimes even graphic detailed images that the reader is swept along and taken over by whatever experience, anecdote or memory she describes. The most accessible poems, and perhaps the most moving, are her family poems dealing with earlier generations, her own generation and the generation to come – which are sprinkled through the collection.

Childhood, as in the other collections, is also a theme. Yet there is none of Oswald's pretentiousness or coyness here. 'At the Balancing Lakes' is a memory that stands out in her childhood: of 'the tallest girl' in her class nearly drowning. The tension builds up until this girl is 'bouncing/ on an underwater/ trampoline but slowing down'. We are then diverted to Morrissey herself as a girl, but the final little scene shows us the tall girl again vomiting, recovering from her near-drowning. Another poem, 'My Life According to You' is written in deliberately childish, simplistic language, but this is not for any superficial effect; it is appropriate as the 'you' is presumably her child, and it is the child's version of her life that she records. This poem, too, is divided into separate little scenes or chapters in each verse, giving the reader a potted, personal biography as the child views it. The lack of punctuation aids the speed of the prose which is the speed of her life which even continues into unlived years, when the child-narrator has grown up with his/her own family, everything in its time.

Her somewhat satirical view of a primary school's Nativity play mocks the Principal who 'occupies his moment/ so deliberately he might be chairing Congress'. We all know the type, and also recognise the conformity of the 'row of just-licked-by-a-cow-looking boys/ in dressing gowns'! In the poem 'Perfume', which has no full stops, her Great Aunt Winnie with her 'rollered hair', has 'trudged in' to Nottingham's Odeon Cinema 'to sweep and mop/ and dust the flip-back seats' when she finds a crack in the cinema floor. This poem skilfully captures the whole era of Beatle mania in the '60s. Yet the poem springs a surprise towards its end as the crack, surrealistically, grows bigger and divides the North from the South of England, and mothers from daughters, 'the chasm between them strung/ with brilliant washing' – demonstrating the generation gap.

The six-part poem, 'The Collier' (her grandfather who loved betting on racehorses) is memorable.

> ... he'd rely on the tug-at-his-sleeve of instinct:
> his grandmother's Romany nous with horses, his blacksmith-
> father's apprising sense bred into his muscles and veins...

I could quote so much from this poem – his life down the mine, 'an auditorium', when he'd eat only bread and jam sandwiches and cold tea; his marriage to her granny after an accident down the pit; his convalescence in Miner's Rest, the woodbines smoked etc. but it needs to be savoured whole to be fully appreciated.

'The Singing Gates' has the grandfather in it again, this time released from five years inside, 'Tipped out onto the pavement like a sack/ of damaged apples' as the gaol's gates 'clanged shut'. She gives a picture of her grandad walking her father (his son) to the top of Divis hill; he would walk for catharsis, emphasised by the repetition of 'walked': he 'walked to think,/ walked for pleasure, walked to stretch each inch of his cell// by laying it down, over and over, on the floor/ of the borderless world'. As in some of the other poems, different generations are handled well because then the poem shifts to Morrissey, the mother, with her probably dyslexic son, the 'dark-haired// flurry in a hailstorm'

Who can't tell *b* from *d* because any letter might just flick

its Fred Astaire hat and dance backwards across the page...

Shift back to the Grandad with his son, and the arresting simile, the 'clouds passing over their faces like zeppelins'. The poem ends with the scattering of the grandfather's ashes by all the remaining generations, and then, in the territory of Burnside and Berry, we are back to the gates, the singing gates:

Are they, in fact, the singing ticket to the afterlife

And how might we post ourselves into it, limb by limb?
What scarab? What amulet? What feather? What scale? What spell?

'Wheel of Death' is a brilliant, exhilarating poem about a visit to Ireland's famous Duffy's Circus. The near diamond shapes of the stanzas replicate little canvas circus tents pitched in the wet mud, and the rhyming, or near rhyming (with assonance, consonantal rhyme, full rhyme or half rhyme) of the first two lines of every stanza invite us in to the performances, where, with the awning unsteady because battered by the wind, 'balancing abilities get tendered/ recklessly, out to us/ as a final sacrifice'. With what seems like a fall: 'a slip/ in your forward flip', 'gravity's/ lack of mercy' is proved.

The penultimate poem, 'The Rope' again demonstrates her talent for form. The second and fourth lines in every stanza employ different sorts of rhyme indicating, I think, her rhyming with her children, who themselves are suddenly rhyming with each other – and their possible futures. Hidden, she watches her young children suddenly discover that they are good friends, aged eight and six, and this is the 'surprise' gift of the summer to her. This poem is a wonderful paean to childhood's magic:

> You whirl and pirouette, as in a ballet,
> take decorous turns, and pay for whatever you need
> with a witch's currency

She sees thicken their 'sibling-tetheredness, an umbilicus,/ fattened on mornings like this as on a mother's blood,/ loose, translucent, not yet in focus', yet 'already strong enough/ to knock both of you off your balance/ when you least expect it'. She continues to imagine the pair of them as adults with their own families and lives – when the rope tugs them back into the present moment and they resume their play, but without her watching.

All five poets, with varying degrees of success, are wordsmiths, and it is to be hoped that the best of them will last forever as, in Michael Longley's words, 'moth-and-butterfly-wing decipherers'.

W S Milne

Ad Terminus

Tony Curtis: *From The Unfortunate Isles: New and Selected Poems* (Seren, 2016)
Elaine Feinstein: *The Clinic, Memory: New and Selected Poems* (Carcanet, 2017)
Mike Sharpe: *Getting There: Late Poems* (Small Press Publishing, 2016)
Jeremy Hooker: *Ancestral Lines* (Shearsman Books, 2016)
C. K. Williams: *Falling Ill* (Bloodaxe Books, 2017)
Helen Dunmore: *Inside The Wave* (Bloodaxe Books, 2017)
Clive James: *Injury Time* (Picador, 2017)

Helen Dunmore has written that Tony Curtis's poems 'reverberate with present, sensuous experience' (this is evinced, for example, in a line such as 'Rich and gold, the wheat settled like hair') and in his Introduction to his book Curtis says 'friends in the visual arts have inspired ideas', clearly seen in those poems where the poet writes with a photographer's eye: there are many references to cameras in the volume – see especially the poem on the American O. Winston Link ('Villanelle for a Photographer'). 'Home' is a keyword for Curtis (he likes the symbol of homing pigeons, for instance) and home for him is Wales, placing himself firmly in the Welsh tradition, quoting Idris Davies approvingly: 'Make us, O Lord, a people fit for poetry', an injunction his own work fittingly enacts. His provenance is everyday realities – pigeon racing, phone calls, deaths, funerals, children learning to swim – and the way in which they mell and clash in an almost cinematic way:

> If I open my left eye the camera squint blurs
> and is over-ridden by the widening garden:
> potatoes flowering, a line of crisping clothes,
> a ragged towel holed, through which the sky shows...

Ecology is a principal theme, conservation in the Wendell Berry mode, how the natural world seems all out of kilter, man now the deadly Leviathan, laying waste the whales' 'ancient guts', a world given over to 'factory ships' and 'fat tankers'. Poetry for Curtis is seen as a 'pitch of water in the desert', 'healing waters' that can help put this imbalance right, surmounting what he calls 'the commonwealth of prose', the ubiquitous empiricism of the modern world. There are poems here on war (e.g. 'Home Front', 'Pro Patria', and 'For Queen and Country') and the horrors of the concentration camps (see 'The Visit to Terezin') but the bulk of the volume is taken up with the subjects of art and poetry (see especially in this regard the sequence 'Arches', poems in response to collages by John Digby, helpfully reproduced alongside the poems themselves). 'Oh, bless the world with colour', 'Oh, paint and write and play, old men' Curtis writes, preparing the way for eulogies and elegies on Gwen John, Dannie Abse, Dylan Thomas, David Jones, William Orpen, Graham Sutherland, Hans Theo Richter, B. S. Johnson, Peter Prendergast, Iwan Gwyn Parry, and John Knapp Fisher. There is something painterly (in a positive sense) about Curtis's poetry. In his own words, he is 'startled by the visible', praising people, places, birds and flowers, relishing Welsh place-names in particular.

To my mind the best poems in the collection are the one's memorialising his father (particularly the one entitled 'The Weather Vane'), dealing with his memory tactfully and gently:

> The last light's fallen away.
> There's no man or paddles or wishing well.
> You and I separated by a long year,
> going our own ways into the second year.

The finest poem of all is one entitled 'Letting Go' (borrowed from the Emily Dickinson poem) which contains the arresting line: 'old women laying their bones against white sheets.' The theme of death or dying is foregrounded in a number of poems here, all of them striking and convincing. Curtis is a poet well worth reading. One point to note for future editions of this work: there is a printing error on page 27. The footnote is on the wrong page.

Fiona Sampson has written that Elaine Feinstein's poetry is 'emotionally intelligent' and 'observant', which is true, but I think Ted Hughes was nearer the mark when he talked of her 'sinewy' style, a toughness, a ruggedness that enables her to be both truthful and fearless, qualities especially necessary in her recent poems dealing with her serious illness. She is very honest about dwelling in a world of hospital visits, piss pots, oxygen masks, asthmatic spasms, failing eyesight, no longer able (or allowed) to drive, learning to walk again with a stick, feeling unsafe in the shower, wig-fitting after chemotherapy, counting pills, checking blood-sugar levels and blood pressure, discarding syringes, listening to machine-beeps and losing her hair – a bleak litany of woes. The whole effect is one of the patient feeling superannuated, starting to look like her mother, she says, aging rapidly and recalling 'lifelong friendships long since over'. The effects of this process are memorably felt by the reader of these very moving poems. The title echoes Nabokov's memoir *The Onion, Memory*, but in this case Feinstein feels that hindsight is not a disappearing act but a quality closer to healing:

> Too many friends are gone, from every
> page of my life, and there is even
>
> something treacherous in me, almost
> consenting to the whisper of a gentle voice
>
> saying – *weaker by the day, but not in pain,*
> *and reconciled to dying – sooner rather than later...*

In this extreme condition the poet says 'nothing is stranger than the habit of prayer' (and the reader intimates that poetry comes into the same category) but writing gives her the strength to continue, 'winning through' as she says, to poetry, the poems coming as 'unexpected gifts'. In this way she finds herself 'making sense of being alive', awaiting death that even Houdini couldn't escape (see the poem entitled 'Houdini's Last Trick'), defeating what she calls 'the seasons of the mortal', living on, one hopes, through one's work:

> Every day won from such
> darkness is a celebration
> 						(from 'Getting Older')
>
> Late summer. Sunshine. The eucalyptus tree.
> It is a fortune beyond any deserving
> to be still *here*, with no more than everyday worries,
> placidly arranging lines of poetry.
> 						(from 'Long Life')

So there is no sense of bitterness or rancour, only a life-affirming tone, especially with regard to the memory of her husband and the delight she takes in her children and grandchildren. The poems commemorating her husband's illness are particularly fine (see all the poems selected from the volume *Talking to the Dead*):

> I drive imagining you still at my side,
> wanting to share the film I saw last night,

of wartime separations, and the end
when an old married couple reunite.

You never did learn to talk and find the way
at the same time, your voice teases me.
Well, you're right, I've missed my turning,
and smile a moment at the memory,

always knowing you lie peaceful and curled
like an embryo under the squelchy ground,
without a birth to wait for, whirled
into that darkness where nothing is found.
(from 'Winter')

The collection also contains elegies to Sylvia Plath, Isaac Rosenberg, Anna Akhmatova, Yehuda Amichai, Herman Melville, Louis Armstrong, Jean Rhys, Edith Piaf, Miroslav Holub, Elizabeth Bishop, and Nadezhda Mandelstam, poems that place grief in a more universal context. In addition, there are excellent poems on her years studying at Cambridge (entering 'the Christian centuries with Donne and Herbert' as she phrases it), her Russian ancestry, the diaspora ('Scattering'), and her beloved London (in a poem of that name addressed to her grandchild Natasha):

Have you seen London from above? She asks me.
It is like a field of lights. And her grey eyes widen.
Her eight-year-old spirit is tender as blossom.
Be gentle to her now, ferocious London.

This is a sketch only of what the book offers. The whole book is haunting, but the true depths can only be appreciated by reading the poems themselves. In her biography of Ted Hughes, Elaine Feinstein argued that 'some poets struggle for a lifetime to find their own voice… Ted Hughes found his early on'. I think this is true also of Elaine Feinstein's own poetry.

Mike Sharpe appears to have reached that age when one spends more time looking back than forward, when memory comforts and the future appals. Comfort is to be found in family life ('It is their accomplishment/to crown my retrospective show' he writes) and love in old age is 'deep-rooted' he tells us, evoking a sense at last of 'getting there', of finding peace. The 'ceremony' of a wedding makes 'sense of things/that are too fugitive to see' in 'these late years'. Memory, recollection, is likened to 'picking flowers', 'raking over old earth' in 'these contemplative slow days' of old age. Although he admits there are regrets, 'what-ifs', he finds solace in the writing of poetry, 'to make discoveries/that would outlast… the slow decay' of old age. Spring still has its attractions for him, 'as days grow longer and the sun is warm'. He discovers 'the world is blessed' through what he terms 'the discerning structure' of a poem, each day 'a ritual/that's meant to take away the fear'. At this time of his life, he says, he finds himself easily moved to tears, 'compassion comes unchecked', feeling at one with 'winter's edge'. *Getting There* is a gentle, humane pamphlet, with something to constantly interest the reader. The compressed scale of the lyric suits the poet, concentrating emotion in just the right way, the poems as a sequence forming a whole.

The cover of Jeremy Hooker's book informs us that *Ancestral Lines* is a sequence of poems about 'the river of desire that flows through the lives of a family'. Hooker describes his poetry as a 'lyric of being', the title of an essay he appends to the collection, defining it as 'the quick of experience, whether felt or glimpsed: the living moment which, in an image, may intimate the whole life it is part of'. And this seems just about right, especially in regard to a family narrative of which he himself forms a part, making, as he quotes David Jones as saying, 'a shape out of the very things of which one is oneself made'. He adds, I think convincingly, 'but even after death we continue to influence others both genetically and through whatever we leave', his own inheritance the poems he writes which he calls 'new fragments of ruined lives':

> As I gave their ashes
> to river and sea, so
> for want of a memorial
> I give this back to them…

Hooker in his verse has a rare sense of community. He argues: 'we exist by virtue of relationships… Life only exists because it is shared', 'as if memory were in the very air, in the colour and texture of pavements, houses, trees, fields.' The poems creatively enact this belief, following what he calls the 'web' of family history in a way reminiscent of Fleur Adcock's 2014 volume *The Land Ballot*:

> voices of the river,
> of the sea and its tides,
> voices that sound with other voices
> in my mind, mixing
> with what I remember, what I am told,

fact becoming story,
story becoming myth,
myth becoming part of us,
moulding our lives…

The poet charts memories of World War Two , of learning words as a child, but most of all he dwells on old age, its 'dark forms looming', dreams gone, dissipated, 'the broken walls of a house lie/scattered in shingle and sand'. But, as with Mike Sharpe, there is a hopeful sense that poetry redeems the day, still 'trying to find the words' late in life: 'through all/the blood streams,/ turbulent, dark/shaping new worlds'. In this way evanescence, transience ('nothing fixed,/invisible signatures/on field and river and wood') can be surmounted, a debt repaid as a gift. Time's drift, its inexorability (its 'frozen pool'), can be overcome:

Forgotten,
Aubrey and Ivy,
no more than ash or bone,
the home emptied,
the house filled with other lives.

This sense of community is recovered partly through the poet's genealogy-hunting (see especially the section called 'Evans'). But the past remains 'unreadable', 'the sheer quick of life' that is the family history of professional gardeners has gone, and the poet in old age feels 'the sheer quick' of life going, his energy sapped, the joy of 'sheer livingness' fading. Still he goes on, his head 'filled with words', still 'learning to see'. Jeremy Hooker's style is unforced and natural, concealing a deft, controlled craft. The poems of *Ancestral Lines* are those of an accomplished writer.

The American poet C. K. Williams passed away in 2015. *Falling Ill* tracks the course of his terminal illness, a type of diary of his last days. These poems he calls 'a way to cry goodbye', imagining his imminent end: 'Whenever it will be it will be *now*/its *own* now', testifying to a feeling of hopelessness, 'as though one might close one's eyes and/chant *life*', a desperate kind of prayer. The terror of impending death is evoked, with the longing for it without the pain:

Silent death hangs slackly faded bare
I feel against me with abiding terror
as it offers my own ignorance to mock me

There are poems here about being depressed, crying, about 'bad' days and 'good' days, about staggering, lurching, swaying, tottering, reeling, falling, tumbling, trembling, losing mobility. There are poems about doubt and fear ('to verify whether I'm breathing as I should/if my heart is beating as it should'), about feeling cowardly ('what are you moaning about voice my voice'), about waking up asking 'am I still here/though I'm not certain whom I'm asking/or what I'm still looking for out there' ('Everyone'), about 'granite memories' and 'acid memories', 'the sludge and scum' of the past.

The impressive aspect of this volume is its bravery of tone; there is no hint of sentimentality or mawkishness about Williams's poems. He thinks of friends who have died: 'Those of you who've gone before how precious/ you remain', remembering them in a rhythm borrowed from Thomas Hardy, 'how you might be other than you ever were'. He is ever aware of 'death's advent', of creeping lethargy and slow-wittedness, alive now he feels 'only in vaults of memory'. There is impatience with 'gullible hope', with punctuated periods of feeling 'better', feeling 'worse', with his rage, frustration, anger, and even with the doctors who 'keep him going', 'fighting for his life'. He just 'wants to get it over with'. Despondency triumphs, and all comforting clichés fail: 'my bones and my living flesh turning to stone'. With 'death drawing closer' he adopts strategies to keep himself 'from being afraid', thinking back on his youth 'radiant with hope', but then a catalogue of medicines and drugs intervenes, jolting him back into 'the lurch' of dying and a realisation of the body's 'guttering flame'–the need to keep track, almost obsessively, of his pathological condition, his body letting him down with its aches and pains and twinges. At all times in this sequence Williams feels mortality pressing ('hurtling to oblivion' as Geoffrey Hill called it in his late poems), encompassed as he is by X-rays, plastic bottles of urine, scans and operations (as in Elaine Feinstein's book), the whole process leading him towards humiliation and degradation. He hates his increasing dependency on others, his frailty, the diagnoses, prognoses and the finessed nuances medics appear to cherish between the meaning of 'symptoms', 'conditions' and 'maladies', and their seeming indifference to the fact that he himself knows he is dying. The intensity of the sequence is at times deliberately comical in its brash extremism, somewhat akin to a Woody Allen film (one thinks of Allen's famous quip: 'I don't mind dying; I just don't want to be there when it happens!'). This mixing of humour with pathos is very effective. In the closing of a life, the poetry of isolation breaks through to reach the reader. The book is very moving.

Helen Dunmore has the eye of an experienced novelist ('all ways to catch the world' as she phrases it) and we find this quality demonstrated clearly in *Inside The Wave*, her latest volume of poems. That expert eye is now focused on the subject of her own illness and the painful sight of a loved one dying, surrounded by painkillers, sharing in what she tenderly calls 'a company of suffering':

> I have never known you easily
> Hold my hand as you do now.
> We sit here for hours....
> I hold your hand and say nothing.
> Once I must have held
> Your finger, a loose curl...
> The ice is so fragile
> You must spread your weight, like this
> And inch out to the abyss...

There is fear of annihilation ('darkness/crossing you out in a swipe') tempered by the poet's vigil: 'the lit candle,/the pain, the breath of my people/Drawn in pain'. Caring for a loved one in hospital she notes 'I hear your breath, now failing', relishing their words, 'the one word that flows from the lips/And the one heart by which it is heard/Unrepeatable, fragile' (from 'In Praise of the Piano') confirming the communion of love. But death is never very far away in this book, caught in the distinctive image: 'There is a gargoyle look when the mouth caves'.

Dunmore writes of her own experience in hospital, of being 'hooked to oxygen' awaiting an operation, thinking of still relevant myths ('a wild/Nest of old stories' as she calls them in the poem 'Odysseus to Elpenor') which manifests respect for the dead as well as the fear of dying, in Aeneas' visit to Hades, for example, the poet (and Virgil too, one intimates) 're-opening the old mines', 'to go below/The bare bright surface' to the dark essence of things, unearthing 'the rare metals' of life. Like Mike Sharpe, Dunmore has reached that age when she has 'more acquaintance/Among the dead than the living'–and when she finds herself counting backwards on the operating table she tells herself 'you can get used to everything', as she gets to grips with the everyday realities of aging and illness. Here craft and emotion coalesce, always a test of a poem's credibility.

The translations of Catullus contained in the volume are fine enough, but there is something wrong with the one entitled 'The Babel of Nations', based on 'Multas per Gentes', one of the most famous elegies ever written. The last line of the Latin reads 'atque in perpetuum, frater, avē atque vale' ('hail, brother, and farewell, forever'). Dunmore paraphrases this in a very curtailed fashion as 'What else can I give?/Only a last greeting.' This tone appears to entertain some kind of hope, where there is none to be had: 'in perpetuum' could hardly be more final. But this is mere carping, the other translations explore new possibilities from old models, and are of a piece with the excellence of the rest of the book.

We come now to Clive James' *Injury Time*, a title which comes a little second-hand, the phrase having been turned to good account by Geoffrey Hill in his 1998 volume *The Triumph of Love* (describing himself there as a 'Rancorous, narcissistic old sod' and going on in the third person to ask, 'So how much more does he have of injury time?'). In some ways this is an unfortunate clash, but it does not detract from the value of James's book. 'Injury Time' follows on from the 'extra time' of James's 2015 book of poems *Sentenced to Life* which dealt with his emphysema and kidney failure ('dying by inches' as he described it in that volume). The cover to *Injury Time* tells us James finds himself 'with more time on the clock than he had anticipated', the poet informing the reader that 'my confidently forecast imminent demise turned out not as imminent at all', describing himself as 'an exhausted footballer still plugging away with legs like lead'. The dedication to the book expresses his gratitude to the nurses, doctors and staff of Addenbrooke's Hospital in Cambridge 'with all my thanks for these unexpected recent years.' He is very grateful he has not yet 'downed tools' as he expresses it, relishing the irony in the title of the opening poem, 'The Return of the Kogarah Kid'. The poet still has a sting in his tail.

James writes in *the Review* mould (he comes out of the same nineteen-sixties' stable as Ian Hamilton, Martin Dodsworth, Colin Falck, and Hugo Williams) writing in short, plain-speaking poems that nearly often rhyme, which I for one find very encouraging and refreshing given the plethora of free verse one has found latterly on bookshop shelves (that is when one can find the poetry section at all). James writes without any sense of grumbling, neuroticism or hysterics, facing his approaching death with an admirable stoicism:

> Soon there will be
> Only one final thing left to occur,
> One little thing. You need not fear for me:
> It can't hurt. Of that much I can be sure.
> I know the place. I have been there before.

He faces what Fleur Adcock has called 'the scariest journey of all' with great bravery, lamenting at the same time what he is about to lose ('I do not wish to leave yet' he says in a deeply-felt phrase –'I liked it here' is a *cri de coeur* I found very moving in its naturalness, its frankness). The book is the poet's way of saying goodbye to his loved ones before verbal cohesion leaves him, when words 'finally fail' and senescence triumphs. It is what he terms, with a fine mix of pathos and humour, 'his dying fall.' I enjoyed the line 'At this rate I will still be here in the spring', echoing Samuel Beckett's Malone: 'I would not put it pass me to pant on to the Transfiguration.'

What I like most about this book (and the previous collection, *Sentenced to Life*) is how the author still grips on to life with all its wonders. Each day is still looked forward to ('The new tide always ready to begin', 'Darkness gave the dawn/Its inward depth') even though 'the power of hope runs wild' and 'strength is sunk so low.' The phrase 'the Himalayan slog upstairs to bed' says it all, but there is joy in the fact that he comes 'back down next morning, still not dead.' I particularly like the Prospero-tone of 'all our travels must come to rest/In stillness' (he is aggrieved that he cannot travel home to Australia), a feeling that he has lived life to the full. I like his sense of hope, of continuity: 'The old ones disappear, the young dance on'. There is a compact lyricism here rarely found in verse today. He is very realistic about his failing powers ('I might not/Summon the strength to see the season through') yet he has the optimism to hope that he will remain part of his granddaughter's 'memory/Each time the comedy of life strikes her/As wonderful' as he moves downward to 'the dying voice of silence', the awaiting 'abyss'. I like the way in his poem 'Recollected in Tranquillity' (a far cry from what Wordsworth intended) he self-deprecatingly mocks himself by talking of 'reprieve', only to be told by the medics that it is no such thing at all, only a 'delay'!

It comes home to James then that he is only the 'old crock with the stoop'; life's 'candy windows' (see the poem of that title) have become real glass now. We see the poet getting over bouts of pneumonia, dealing with new drugs and their side-effects, death now 'a slow-loping fury'. Dullness, lassitude, weight loss and muscle-wastage take up much of his time, whilst he is thankful still he can still breathe just enough to smile! I like the way James celebrates such small victories.

The nursing-home may loom but the poet is still here, still 'strutting his stuff'. Words for him are 'the joy-spring of language', enabling him to recall life's generous 'sprawl', trying to forget the moment 'When there is no more dying to do/And I am burned and poured in a jar.'

These are poems one wishes to return to again and again, a sure sign of worth. The poet holds onto images of daily order, affirming his humanity which aims (as he once argued himself in an early essay on the poetry of Elizabeth Bishop) beyond mere precision, transcending the bravura of craft, to give us moving, engaging poems. James possesses a poet's sense of his medium, to a marked degree. His poems overturn the (mainly modernist) notion that art must be impersonal. In the closing of a life, as with C.K. Williams, his poetry breaks through isolation, reaching out to the reader – in this way *Injury Time* presents us with some of the finest poems about hospitalization and illness since Fleur Adcock's 'The Soho Hospital for Women' (in *Inner Harbour*, 1979) and Grey Gowrie's *The Domino Hymn: Poems from Harefield* (2006).

The overall effect of reading these seven books is to admire the courage required of the authors to face the indignities of aging and dying. Illness sits, waiting to bloom, the sufferers living on borrowed time, dwelling in what Susan Sontag termed 'the kingdom of the sick'. The authors (or others they love) are enduring chronic illness, pain, discomfort, humiliation, vexation and at times embarrassment, seeking sympathy, hoping for relief, that something can be done to alleviate their fear and suffering, the hope that they might survive a while longer, trying not to think on 'the bitter little of life that remains' (in Robert Burns's fine phrase). In modern life we all seem to shy away from illness and death as much as we can, and dread old age, 'the cane, the wrinkled hand, the special chair' as Edna St Vincent Millay put it. It is to the great credit of all the writers above that they face the issues head-on, without flinching, honest in their apprehensions. 'Dying is an art' Sylvia Plath wrote, 'like everything else'. And her words are certainly appropriate here. Only by finding the right words, the right rhythms, have these poets managed to look death in the eye, and praise what we all love best: life itself.

It is often said that poetry lacks a public voice. These books disprove the view, obdurately and magnificently. They redeem poetry in an age which seems hell-bent on destroying everything we value as human, showing us that verse is something we all need. Perhaps Keats was right after all when he wrote, 'Sure a poet is a sage; a humanist, a physician to all men'– poetry bringing comfort when all else fails.

*

Very sadly, we have to report the death of Helen Dunmore (reviewed here) on June 5th, 2017. May this journal be a tribute to the very fine poet and person that she was.

Requiescat in Pace

Shanta Acharya

Truth's 'superb surprise'

Carol Rumens: *Animal People* (Seren, 2016)

Animal People, the latest collection by the award-winning poet Carol Rumens, alters our understanding of the scope of poetry, not just our appreciation of her work. Her first poem, 'On Standby', where having 'tasted words', one is left in no doubt of her vocation – reminded me of Mark Doty's 'Eating Poetry'. And in the last, 'On the Spectrum', she explores from a female perspective, partly from her own life, what it is to be 'on the autistic spectrum' as poetic documentary. Along the way we make our personal journeys and discoveries that enhance our view of what poetry is. Her writing, in the words of Anne Stevenson, 'testifies to the generosity of her imagination and to the persistence of her dedicated wrestle with words and meaning.' Rumens' many awards include the Alice Hunt Bartlett Prize, a Cholmondeley Award and the Prudence Farmer Prize.

In 'On Standby', she begins with: 'Pass me that small pencil, sharpened nicely/ At both ends, a pencil with two eyes, And up for anything – a screed, a scribble.' Mining images from diverse sources, she defines her craft: 'A pencil starts from scratch, like anyone./ It knows hard graft, despair and knuckled tension, /A shadow flickering like a footballer's – / Designed for transfer.' Then towards the end, she lets slip: 'If you've never/ Nibbled at a pencil-top, you've never/ Tasted words.' This interweaving of experiences – childhood, writing, school, play, football, computers, self-discovery – is strikingly refreshing. Her poems entertain as much as they educate, challenging established ways of seeing the world, unsettling our prejudices. 'Poets must tell the truth,' she reminds us in 'Easter Snow'. And like Emily Dickinson, Rumens lets the truth's 'superb surprise' sink in unobtrusively.

The author of sixteen collections of poems in addition to fiction, drama, translation, a collection of her poetry lectures, she has also edited a number of anthologies and journals. Having taught at the Universities of Kent (Canterbury), Queen's (Belfast), University College (Cork), Stockholm and Hull, Rumens is currently Visiting Professor in Creative Writing at the University of Bangor. A Fellow of the Royal Society of Literature, she is editor of 'Poem of the Week' for *The Guardian*, where her brilliant analysis of the weekly poem is as much a treat for the reader as her chosen poem, validating a line in one of her own poems, 'Footnote' 'Canto XXVII, Purgatorio, *The Divine Comedy*, Dante': 'to be taught is to be fed.'

Rumens' richly layered poems are widely admired for their technical brilliance, subtlety of subject matter and intensity of thought – be it a 'Glosa on *Woman of Spring* by Joan Margarit' or 'The Reddish Wheel-Barrow'. It is perhaps not surprising to discover poems in *Animal People* inspired by translations ('Three Fado' 'freely, from the Portugese', 'Laundry Blue' 'freely after Attila József', or 'The Ship of the State' 'After Brodsky, after Horace, translated from the Russian with Yurji Drobyshev', her late partner) reflecting her grasp of several languages. Sometimes she and Yura (her name for her partner, to whose memory *Animal People* is dedicated) worked together on translations, but in 'Hamlet', subtitled 'freely after Boris Pasternak', she embarks on her own, turning her poem into a sonnet, experimenting with words and form, British slang not excluded. Her re-readings of classic works of literature (for example, 'The Teacher and the Ghosts after *A Christmas Carol* by Charles Dickens' or 'The Hare and the Hedgehog') reinforce the extent of her engagement with words and ideas. Besides, her range is formidable – includes history, politics, mythology, philosophy, science and more. Executed in her distinctive style, Rumens' poetry is a fine balance of wit and learning, her seriousness belied by a lightness of tone.

The inclusion of words and phrases from different languages (Welsh, Irish, Yorkshire, Russian) enrich her canvas as they seem to come naturally. By defining them in her poems she is able to draw upon centuries of culture and tradition, each language a way of living, of seeing the world. 'Spring Forward, Fall Back: A Gwynedd Skein' is an example of how poetry communicates before it is understood:

>   milk-tooth   eirlys
>   an earth-cub's yawn
>
>   soaked his black fur
>   beneath iâ du
>
>   frost on our ffos
>   by noon
>   frogspawn

The notes at the bottom of the page inform us that 'Spring Forward, Fall Back' is mnemonic for BST clock-adjustments, 'eirlys' is snowdrop, 'iâ du' black ice and 'ffos' ditch. Never striking a false note, her delight in words is palpable, her images and metaphors linger on in memory. Here are a few examples:

>   wrinkled as tortoises, so shy and slow,
>   we'd never kissed. We'd never said hello.
>   (Remote Bermudas – 3. The Campus of Time-Enough)

> The shyest grass aims upwards,
>
> but the ways of the insects
> are horizontal.
>
> Like us, they are slow kissers.
>   ('Fire, Stone, Snowdonia')

> But God who hadn't started anything, seemed newly plausible.
>   ('The Big Bang Year')

> 'Bees are scarfed in gold   the goldfinch misted silver'
>   ('Praying with the Imam at Summmerfade')

> '...*if you're a woman you just have to grow and grow.*'
>   ('Happy Seventieth Birthday Blues, Mr Zimmerman')

Some of her poems deal with the art of writing, of the poet's relationship with words:

> Wind in the silence. Words. I sometimes meet them.
> They never begin by asking for a light,
>
> never return a text; they chew their lips
> like stubborn children who confide their day
>
> only if you desist from questioning them,
> or else keep up a stare
>
> so long you see the first pond-water eye
> hair-pricked by sunbeams, pinned until it seeps
>
> a retinal cell
> and what it sees would have been called 'amazing'
>
> if any mouth had formed, or any mouthing.
> When word-suns shine, it's not philosophy.
>   ('A Few Study-Notes')

In her poem, 'On the Spectrum' she speaks of 'metaphors, slipped rind,/ one twisted-metal star-collision mirroring your mind.'

And even when she is having fun with words, a world of ideas is never far behind. In 'House Clearance' she explores the notion of humans turning 'into our possessions.' 'Let's just be jars,' she suggests, 'glass, empty, unlabelled,/ fully recyclable.' In a few words she captures her view of the world, as it should be.

In 'The Homeless Ship', subtitled 'seen from the Bangor-Chester train', the ship in a dry dock is a metaphor for the hardships of poverty experienced by many in Wales. Rumens' poem captures in five compact 3-line stanzas the helplessness, the waiting for things to change, the death of hope. She describes a 'Coastline of caravans, neat as graves, but quieter', 'A factory fizzles dry, the land reverts to grazing,/ and there's our ship, beached, ruminant, rusting.'

In the 'Song of the Obsolete' she expresses a similar sense of loss and devastation, poverty and exploitation. With the deft use of repetition and alliteration the poem builds up to its rhetorical climax. The poem begins with:

> Once there was much to be made, much to be made, much to be made,
> Much to be sold to be sold to be sold;
> Much to mix, mash, mould, much to split, splice, spoil, much to catch, much to carry

And ends with:

> *Where are bastards that built us, the slaves that skilled us –*
> *The pay-packer packer, the docker with dockets, the stacker of profits, the stockist?*
> *What are our hours, now it's time that maims and mills us?*

These two studies of life in Wales today are comparable to the best of Dickens or Hugo. A powerful indictment of capitalism, her unforgettable portraits of the state of the nation, captured in a few brilliant strokes, should be read by all – politicians, economic planners, pundits, bankers and industrialists included.

Her humanity is all embracing. One encounters a deep sense of commemoration in this collection. She writes about time passing and the challenges of mortality. 'Home Thoughts from the Cowshed' is a moving tribute to her Yura as she redefines notions of home, foreignness: 'Both of us were blow-ins/ but you, by dying here, became a native.' 'In Memory of a Rationalist', a poignant love poem, the poet observes him lying 'dressing-gowned among his arguments,/ dying, pitiless'. In 'Small Facts' she writes candidly about death:

> I shall not re-make
> my snow-man beliefs,
> nor think it consolation
> ever that you – or any
> creature in its un-making –
> 'quietly'   'sleeps'.

The key to the title of this collection, *Animal People*, is the final sequence 'On the Spectrum', which 'explores from a female perspective some of the effects and affects of Autistic Spectrum Condition (ASC)', confirms Rilke's statement that 'poetry is about everything'. In 'Happy Christmas, Sister Dympna' Rumens begins with: 'Animals *are* people!' In her note 'About Animal People' she says autistic people 'have an unusual affinity with animals' and the 'ability to form special cross-species relationships is certainly an attractive' attribute. 'We're all animal people in the broader sense', she reminds us.

This poem brings together much of what has gone before: 'You look back at your life,' and 'it's the articulation of the best of what you were.' Moving from childhood to death, her poem is full of tenderness and love, of the smell of life, of the 'solitary, naked, trying/ to be covered by a wind of green kisses'. The ending is utterly moving and the repetition of 'my love is not fitting' makes it a prayer of the '*Unbeloved*':

> It is the *Unbeloved*:
> the truth we have never failed,
> who makest us also immeasurable.
>
> Who art within our syndrome.

Fusing multiple lyric forms, the poem is a meditation on what it means to be human. *Animal People* extends our notion of what poetry is and can do, inviting the reader to return to her poems as they keep yielding new insights. We are indeed in the presence of one of the finest living English poets.

Byron Beynon

Concord of Sound

Tony Conran: *Three Symphonies* (Agenda Editions, 2016)

In 1968 the poet Basil Bunting wrote 'with sleights learned from others and an ear open to melodic analogies I have set down words as a musician picks his score, not to be read in silence, but to trace in the air a pattern of sound that may sometimes, I hope, be pleasing.'

Reading the preface to Tony Conran's *Three Symphonies* he says that for some time he had been 'haunted by the idea of a long poem in several disparate movements like a symphony in music'. There is a sense here of a bond between the two poets, wave-lengths not too dissimilar.

The word symphony derives from Greek, meaning a sounding together or concord of sound, and arguably is the most pure musical form that can be written. I believe that during his lifetime (he died in 2013), Conran's Symphonies (the first, *Day Movements*, appeared as far back as 1967) worked towards this union or concord of sound, using the rhythm of words. Conran's book contains symphonies 7 The Magi, 8 Fabrics (in one movement of sonnets), and 9 Everworlds (including 'Requiem for Robert Graves'), all composed in the period 2004-2007. I remember that in December 2004 I published in a magazine (*Roundyhouse*) I co-edited, a sequence of seven sonnets from Symphony 8, which included Fabrics (which became the untitled sonnet 4), 'Stone Age', 'Fleece', 'Washing the Fleece', 'Dye Plants', 'Penelope' and 'India' with 'Brahamani bulls humped like toast racks-all day /Odd villagers with an hour to spare would meet/ To shed the warp, let fly the scuttling weft.' The sonnets were a work in progress, and numbered sixteen when completed.

I first heard his poems being read aloud by his wife Lesley in February 1982, at the Poetry Society in London, when it was based at Earl's Court. By coincidence, the following day I went along to Keats House in Hampstead, where Basil Bunting sat and read by a table in the Brawne Rooms. Conran also belongs to that same line of Modernists which includes Bunting, MacDiarmid and David Jones.

Born in India in 1931, he spent most of his life in north Wales, settling in Bangor, where he taught at the university. Widely published, he was much admired for the passion behind his writing, as a poet, critic, dramatist and translator of Welsh-language poetry. His *Penguin Book of Welsh Verse* appeared in 1967, with translations from a selection of work from fourteen centuries of poetry from Taliesin and Aneirin, to Waldo Williams and Gwyn Thomas. Through his discovery of Welsh literature he went on to learn the rules of cynghanedd, and wrote poems in English which were based on Welsh metres. His books of essays *The Cost of Strangeness* and *Frontiers in Anglo-Welsh Poetry*, are impressive, stimulating and important works, and his many volumes of poetry include *Life Fund* (1979), *Blodeuwedd* (1989), *Castles* (1993), *The Shape of my Country* (selected poems and extracts 2004), and *What Brings You Here So Late?* (2008).

In his informative and thought-provoking introduction to *Three Symphonies* the poet Jeremy Hooker, a fine critical writer on Anglo-Welsh matters, writes with detachment, insight, and warm sympathy, that Conran's 'modernism acknowledges diverse influences including Eliot and Yeats, Robert Graves and Idris Davies... he used what he found in them creatively... in making poetry of striking originality.' Add to this his knowledge of Welsh poetry dating back to the sixth century to the present day, a fusion of something new and powerful occurred. Hooker guides the reader as he notes 'the symphonies' encyclopaedic form includes everything, from the Big Bang to the present state of the world.' We are taken on a poetical, cultural, and political journey, an unsentimental celebration of 'the gift of life', an exploration of 'the making of the world and all that it contains.'

We hear this in the poem 'Life' (from Symphony 7):

Life

It has taken me time

Wherever life grew first –
In black smokers
Of the rifting seabeds
Where bubbling lavas

Geyser up
Into an airless murk;
Or by breakwaters
The soup of lagoons

Warmed by the Sun, but saved
From the deadly light
Under rock debris
Or buried in mud

– Wherever the thin whiskery
Haze of the protein
Replicators
Crept like rottenness

Into sharp stone
Foul-smelling – but
There were no noses –
The secret changelings,

The cloned effluvia
From whose myriads
Came our breathable air,
Our shielded home...

Came, like locust swarms,
Eventually, us.

Conran also thought of his poetry 'as a dance for the tongue and the vocal chords: ultimately, since tongue and vocal chords don't occur in a vacuum, for the whole body, the whole mind.' In an interview in *The New Welsh Review* with Ian Gregson in 1988, he was asked about the influence of Robert Graves, in the sense of how poetry happens, and how it gets written. Conran replied, 'I think that writing poetry does involve you in a different level of experience, a deep trance-like state. But it depends on the poem. Poems which have a strong rhythmic base and the rhythms takes you along into the darkness... the poem is a stranger to you like a baby'.

In the second movement of the final Symphony 9, there are several poems in memory and in praise of Robert Graves, including 'Dejà Unvisited', 'The Erosion of Everworlds', 'Castle', 'Soldier', 'Oxford 1919', 'Disembarking', 'The Goddess Sings', 'To the Utmost', and 'The Peony'.

The second movement begins with:

Passage to Dejà

i.m. Robert Graves (1895-1985)

Dejà Unvisited

The hill haunted me. Dejà –
One of my everworlds
Whose magical fauna

Sometimes as friends of friends would come
Filling my room
With his last, dumb

Awarenesses, geologically
Slow, a poetry
Speechless as lichen.

My household could have been translated
And I'd only to look out
Through olive groves

To see twilight
Blur the long stairs
Up to the town,

The corner to his home…
And behind me, did I half-hear
Her footsteps

Who 'variously haunts'
This hill,
This island Earth?

  This is a life-affirming book, written with intensity and energy, poems of mystery and beauty, where the personality of the poet enters the vital sinew of each poem. He has, as T.S. Eliot said of the work of James Joyce and David Jones, 'the Celtic ear for the music of words'.

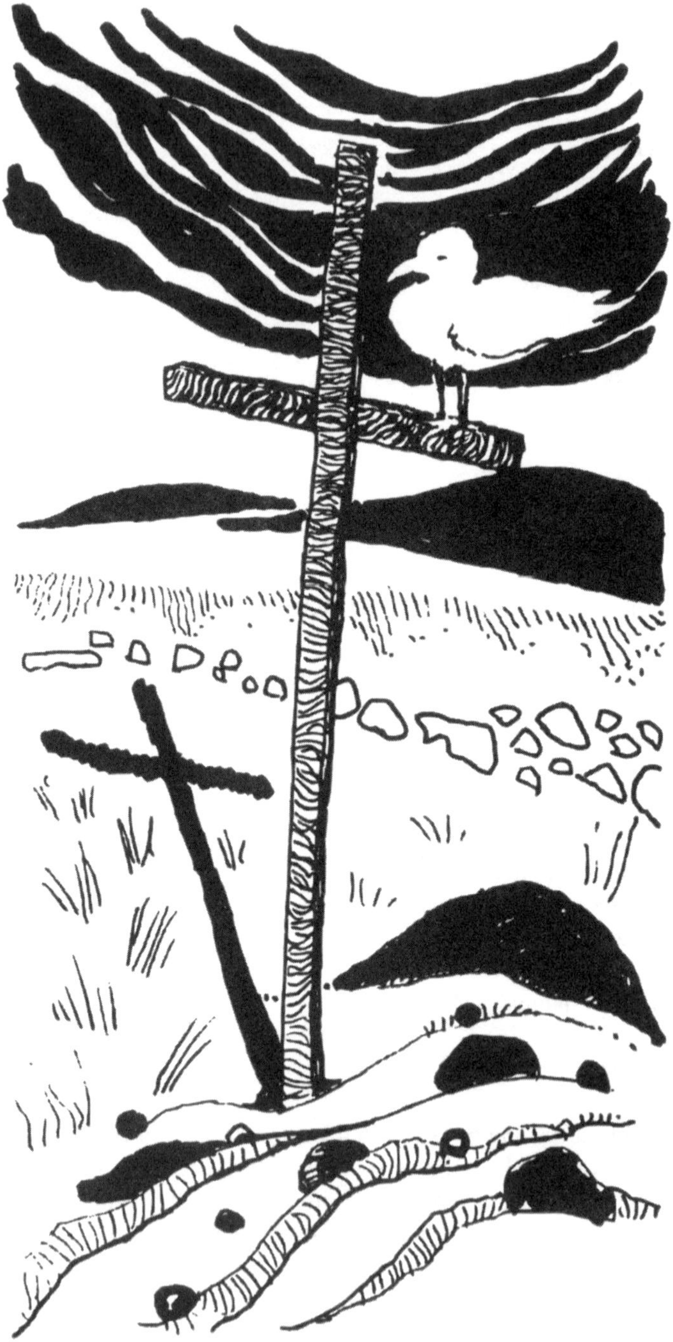

Robyn Rowland

The habit of leaving

(Commissioned by John Carty for his slow air/jig 'Seanamhac Tube Station')

In the 1970-80s the Irish remained the largest immigrant community in Britain. John grew up there and played at the pub 'The Good Mixer'. A multi-awarded Irish traditional musician on fiddle, banjo, flute and tenor guitar he has many albums, solo and accompanied. He wanted a poem to accompany the idea of sadness at leaving, excitement in the journey, as well as the returning… in a short poem!

    There is a story told that when the Irish scholar Sedulius Scottus arrived at a monastery on the continent in the 9thcentury, the abbot Strabo asked why he had left his native land. Was it because of the 'unsettled state of the country or the Irish habit of going away?'

Reared on the water from deep western wells
flowing off faces of ageless rock down through
turf that twines history of trees in its threads, they left.
From autumn lochs slate-slick and sometimes so still
they could almost dance *sean nós* there clacking their heels,
they went out to cities, plains, roads and rails,
to countries quite close or unforseen bays
took with them always music of their own.

Others knew them only by their poverty and song
their language a strange tongue where secrets were stored.
Hearts would cry out for yellow windows of home
and the Bens in their folded blue-velvet haze,
while the *bodhrán* beat out its pulse at the quay
and waves there would drum on the ships' salty planks,
feet jig on the boards tight as strings for the tunes
stamping loss underfoot in the dance of their own.

Trasna na
                    dtonnta

                    dul siar
                    dul siar

Places they drifted to, faraway, anyway,
had their own patterns and ways to their words,
strange in strange places they held one another
remaking village among concrete and smog.
Days hard at toiling, nights filled with drinking,
they sang the old songs and played the old tunes:
London bursting with newness, excitement,
free paths opening, adventure and change.

Trasna na
               dtonnta

        dul amach
        dul amach

They called it in London the *Seanamhac Tube*,
younger the 80s brought less grief more food,
unsettled state or that habit of going away?
Journeymen and women all in our blood
we still go out from hope or from need,
from longing for something other than home
where new risk might bring riches
the mind might fly free.

And the old wail regret while the young look away,
take to the air now, silver wings flying high
as Connemara swallows head out each year,
urgent for their first glimpse of Sahara sand,
African lions, spires of Paris, stones in Rome.
maps printed inside their blood.
A scrimshaw of homescape fine-carved in their bones:
returning as sure as departing again.

Trasna na
        dtonnta

     dul siar
     dul siar

Sunburnt, surprised, or up *Seanamhac tube*,
our wanderers take with them the face of the land

their bodies have lain across in the dark,
the rhythm of bones, a drum in their blood,
the dance of the bow strung through their veins,
They think *Tír na nÓg* they're travelling towards
horizons of gold and forever young, but hidden within,
the call of the stories never grown old,

and the beat that drives them further,
brings them further back home.

Trasna na
dtonnta

dul siar
dul siar

Notes:
Pronounciation:
Seanamhac Shanawok
Trass-na na dhontah dull ah-mahkh dull ah-mahkh –
over the waves   going out going out
Trass-na na dhontah dull sheer dull sheer –
Over the waves   go back go back

Tír na nÓg (tearnanog) mythical land of the forever young

Different ways with love

One breath taken completely; one poem, fully written, fully read,
in such a moment, anything can happen.
            Jane Hirshfield, *Nine Gates: Entering the Mind of Poetry*

Tell me the different words for love in Turkish again,
so I can name this, anchor it in my history, but not his.
He lives in that other country, youth. This
might need a new word, a meaning more complex than
impossible love, *imkansiz aşk*, or a kind of forbidden love,
yasak aşk. No. Find me words that expand loving.

Aşk. That luscious Turkish word for deep love,
makes you want it, even create it, just to be able to say
the word *aşikane*, I am loving you.
I rifle the language and call you, translator, dear friend.
Give me richness where English seems to hand me only 'love'.
A monosyllable like a monoculture can catch its death from blight.

The young woman just married, barely met, had only that.
Walking Çanakkale harbour in the wind after they gave me a lift
I bought them coffee and ice cream and we wrangled English
with google translate, chuckling, her headscarf firmly fixed.
Brimming with happiness, surprised at kindness, suddenly
'I love you' she said, and, 'I too', I replied instantly. *Sevgi*.

What of you, Mehmet, word magician who takes my lines
blending them into your own tongue with grace,
who drinks Raki with me along any waterfront we visit?
Güvenilir bir arkadaş, trusted friend, to be alone with my poems,
change their shape to one I cannot know,
bring them back to me transformed. Love's faith.

What of the painter Korkut who brings the Ney players to canvas,
who raises Sufi spirits into oils, older growing younger,
keeps Ataturk alive, and the dead soldiers?
His multi-coloured palate of knowledge, the glee of his humour
a feast with Yildez' perfect fruit liquors – plum, raspberry, apricot –
her practical ways, quick patience with our childish jokes.

And Meral, in her island hotel who minds me with generous care
as I come weary and kitchen-useless, while she creates banquets.
Lit with a good life, she turns to me with wisdom and for wisdom
so we become entwined in understanding. Then life is less heavy,
lighter even than extra salty sea we swim across at Tuzburnu beach
before soaking in sun, eating village apricots hot from their waiting.

That love is clear – soul friends. In Irish, *anam cara*, in Turkish,
anam yolu? Deep friendship, *delin arkadazler*, long-loving.
Not the love that tears flesh from your bones,
so without the desired one, fires inside never quench,
self melted into the other, all hope after their death, gone.
Tutku. Passion. Cruel love. Once in a lifetime, no more.

This new feeling in the long-numb heart, makes the aging body sing,
alive again in its well-worn carapace. *Sevda*, love with some kind of
sadness in it? Perhaps. *Hayran*, admiration for his youth, language of smiles,
the beauty of his voice reading aloud my poem, your translation,
his eyes burnt-umber, bright-wet? Perhaps *gerçek aşk*, real love,
when we have learned to leave the other be, asking nothing in return.

Note:
Pron: Turkish ş is pronounced sh, so *aşk* becomes *ashk*

Jessica Mookherjee

The Foreigner

He makes a phone call from his desk,
the room has kept the scents of turmeric, milk,
old suitcases, washing powder, coriander.

nam bhavāya cha rudrā cha

He tells her, don't come, *don't disturb
your mother-she's stable, she's fine.* Too much
distance from London to Wales. *Not needed.*

He won't let her collide with his room.
Won't let accusations, built from broken
conversations, overheard long ago, disturb.

Om Kalakala namahya

In the room, thirty years ago, she answered
his long distance call. His voice cracked, performing
his mother's funeral rites in an unknown town.

His daughter, the good child, read weekly shopping lists
to him on the phone, counted up what she'd spent,
reassured him that her mother had taken the pills.

Premarpana, shama darshana, jagajana

He had no magic to charge up wires,
to turn his voice into gentle hands, to rest like static
on her hair, across the miles from Calcutta to Wales.

Her voice, is clipped now, distant, indifferent.
Her curt goodbye jabs, reminds him of her child-voice,
many years ago, reading that shopping list:

turmeric, washing powder, toothpaste, coriander, milk.

The River God's Daughter

His daughter asks him what river-water tastes like
in hell and he foams from his lips –
sings *Mahandi, Godavari, Hugli*

Down stream, near the bank, a mix of fresh water
and salt where the merge occurs, in drift
of moon-spit, all washed up.

He never thought he would have daughters,
never thought a spell would turn him
into Shylock, Indra, Lear –

he never taught them to swim. Her sister sneers
*When rivers die they are re-born as weather,
better burn him at the Estuary.*

He names her Padma, Lotus, Flood, pulls on her hair
as she looks for a husband in the the pull of tides,
but there is too much weather,

sailors blown into thunder, before the River inhales,
cries and spits them into mountains and drops
his daughter into the cracks of earth

as he collects in clouds – looking for sons, and the girl
keeps running, as he hisses of fat
on the Estuary bank, she keeps running,

in tributaries, meanders, rises from her bed, churns,
gets up for work, keeps going, keeps running,
keeps running to the sea.

Becoming British

They scramble in drawers for affidavits, letters, proof of purchase, receipts, invoices. Voices: *Her father was a district judge, Kulna division,* amidst the shouting. Letters: *we need proof of legitimacy of your marriage.* Headlines: *National Worries of Smuggling in Foreign Women.* Whispers: *Her father is a stateless person, his affidavit worthless. He fled from Bengal during the riots, to Dehradun.* What colour is her passport?

In a suitcase, under her saris, she strokes her wedding jewels, old blue airmail letters from her father *You will bring shame on both our families if you don't marry her.* Must be somewhere. The vows she said under the stars, garments tied in flesh-red and bone-white. In Comilla, under the pole star, circling fire and incense smoke, eternity stamped with the priest's thumb, a kick from god. All papers, lost. *We need proof of legitimacy of your marriage.*

Jean Atkin

Dialects of the Coppice

We have come to watch spring write itself
in lithoed tractor tyres.
The fluttering mark of Wood Whites
on the air is unpronounceable.

Here ambiguous deer leave in their mud
the occasional
quotation mark
then dash –

On the track the iron edge of horses
press & pass.
The coppice boles are bold above
the lean italics of grass.

Pond prints out quivered sky.
We can't translate
its soaking scrip of weed.
The trees rephrase the words
the air has shed

& high in the ear we learn
the silences between
the notes of wrens.
Their pauses, language of reply.

Tremulant to swell

a blare of granite sound & then a stealing in
of softness & we drum
soil-deep this prehistoric mound
the mellow thud of bellows held
in the round of churchyard, all
its praying stones

today our heads tipped up to the shining
organ, oak & gold
voicing, *by generous subscription*, all
the singing centuries
now our heads are weighted down
with walls & bells

& pressure of branching columns lifts
a wooden canopy of quiet, while
in the nave our hearts are wrung –
landlocked, we sit & think of tides
as organ bellows like a bull
& treads the shore we fear

to drive a flight of families across
a continent of noise
thins to our fraying *vox humana*
all notes of orange
lifejackets bobbing on the swell
so here's earth's rumble then
the chord that strikes the blow

Mimi Khalvati

The Brag

I am known by sight in the neighbourhood
to shopkeepers, baristas, cab drivers.
There I go, there I come, in likelihood
alone, up and down the road, in all weathers.

I am on smiling terms with hosts of people.
There she blows with her silver hair, they grin,
staking out a beanrow, clearing a table.
Roadsweepers chat, guards greet me at the station.

Some call me lady, auntie, mammy – ask me
how I'm doing, endorse me with endearments,
watch my footing for me, rescue my bag.

Caregivers all! No wonder if I brag
a little, graced with such acknowledgements
and such a large extended family.

The Void

So wide awake is spring now, eyes so open,
even the carpets long to fly outdoors
and prostrate themselves, carpeting the garden.
But is it only sun – bright visitors

from skylights, there, at the top of the stairs,
poised to run down, brass stair rods at their heels;
is it only this sunless room which bears
a weight of shade so sculptural it feels

like Rachel Whiteread's *House* pumped full of concrete;
or is it, not the feeling Jorie Graham
had 'how full void is', but a sense of void,

only the membrane of the void, the sweet
tremble of void itself that casts – O Lord –
the prefaratory glow of a poem?

Iain Britton

from *The Primitives*

#

the poverty of eviction
demands an interpretation | i stand
unassessed | bemused by the depth
of the green forest | the dark gaps
where faces fleetingly appear
where figures stir the undergrowth |
i live receptive to fanged dialects |
naked fighters wrestling with
angels | homeless girls
singing incantatory hymns
from epitaphs on rocks

#

each inbuilt learning ethic
digs deeper | each child stalled
between the minutes | waits for milk
& bread | the gift of fruit | the hands
that care have added me to old
drawings | diagrams | have put me
in a concrete garden for loiterers |
for discarded declarations |
gamblers who tear up others' vanities |
each child is snatched off the street
for his city of gold

John Wheway

Fruit

i

As I pick raspberries, I hardly notice
when thorns prick my fingers, remembering

you, about a year ago, cutting
fennel to garnish the roses on the kitchen sill.

You stood
like a memorial to yourself, gazing

at the faintest of moons.

ii

Tonight
I see only sheep being taken in – trees

in shadow on the field boundaries
losing definition.

Where I find secret pockets of fruit, I forage
deep, the ripest mounting in my bowl,

I exhaust every hiding place – there's so much
I can't bear to waste.

Four raindrops spot
the hazel canopy over my head –

I need
a cloudburst.

iii

In the kitchen, I eat –
it would improve the taste

if I had you at this table, your spoon
chiming on your dish as you lift

raspberries to your lips, juice
escaping, probably, down your chin.

Laurence Wilson

Protection

She'd sniff along this wall, so slowly, slowly...
as eyesight dimmed, it gave her confidence
to have a fence
or wall on one side, me with lead on other.
Slow promenade around the flowered lawn –
the old dog, gone
three-quarters of a year. The melancholy
diminished, dwindled, manageable now.
Remember how
we wept? Remember pain of separation?
Remember ashes spread in churchyard green?
Our furball queen...
I walk here, now and then, and I remember
her mad beginnings and her gentle end,
true-hearted friend.
Sometimes, from cornered eye, I think I see her,
blink-fantasy: white dog, so small, so slow...
oh, yes, I know
she isn't there. She will not lick my fingers
or stretch her legs arthritically and yawn.
The old dog's gone
but memories remain – the wall is solid,
perimeter protecting more than lawn:
our sweet girl, gone

David Ball

The Cemetery Going Down to the Sea

With the wind behind us today from the land
we too might imagine these tombs to be, say,
white sails set to take to the dark blue,
bourgeois family tombs, small houses,
built to last, which prompted the poet
to meditate on transience and uncertainty.

       Yet the waves which break
       Below these ranks of stone,
       Was the music they make
       Heard by him alone?

       Music of sweet despair
       That all must pass and rot,
       Be blown on the salt air
       To the eye's vantage spot.

       So what we came to see
       Is from this point plain,
       And what we strove to be
       Is to begin again.

And again
from places far apart
where poetry has been built upon piety:
the short hard lives lost
beneath the grass they used to tend,
the bones of whalers who will know
no rest from the blood they shed,
from the waves surging to their very graves.

At the Ballet

Six, no, eight Romeos throw wide their arms,
appeal to heaven, the stars, the entire theatre.
The Juliets, at some distance, weave,
dive, skim, float, paper in the wind,
letters tossed on to the stream.
The crescendo: the hero's inner anguish,
a street fight, a crowd scene, a duel...

The dancers' lives are almost as short.
All those girls, each Saturday morning,
how many will come to leap or glide
on to the professional stage?
And for how long? Until,
legs long strings of taut muscles,
knees and ankles both give way,
and they return to the Saturday mornings,
this time as teachers,
in draughty halls, peeling paintwork,
for the next generation of girls.

Danseur: don de soi,
heroes of performance,
subjection of the body,
that what for the dancer is pain,
precision, control,
is for the spectator grace, beauty,
the illusion that the forces of gravity
have for an instant ceased to apply.

Jane Lovell

Eclipse

And there he is
kneeling beside a bucket,
fists clenched in fur until
the useless claws, light as a bird's,
trail away.

Water stills:
an eclipse, a dark lens in a swift sky.

Alone in his lab sifting petri dishes,
a haze of phenol in his clothes.
A scimitar of light.
'Streptococcus'...

He pushes the microscope
towards me.
Sperm-wiggle of nastiness stranded
in bright grease; I hold my breath.

Those hands.
The hand that held the kittens
in cowardly collusion.

I never forgave them, those fingers
now too weak to stir tea.

Night dissolves him.
He crosses the garden, roots to find
a foothold in a shifting landscape,
a world that cannot wait.

I watch his puppet limbs
describe the universe,
with each step flinging away
angels,

arcs of light
across the billowing lawn,
the titanic darkness.

I hear him breathe,
breathe those words:

I want to go first.

Milk

It's all still here:
seascapes of celandine and clover,
trampled earth pooling bitter water,
tremors of shirred light where she stood
scattered and silent

and, way above, a pair of buzzards arcing
and mewling, whirligig larks and their wheedling,
the whole earth and sky swimming in motes
flung from wing and lung, notes carried on the air
seams on a perfect cranium.

Remember her small, determined fingers
working the needle, the mesmerizing thimble,
those boxes of patterns and buttons, bundles
of bright silks to be arranged in rows, to be left
perfectly wound.

Below the oak, cows still sense cloud,
never raise their oilbloom eyes to the cumulus;
bright as algae the spume of cud in their mouths,
those lunging tongues quick as eels.

Dawn and dusk, still they carry their awkward frames
to the clunk and swish of the shed,
the warm milk chugging through an octopus of pipes.

Oblivious to the passing of time longer than day or storm,
they cross the land below the church where once
a dairyman, once a husband, curls in the ground,
ribs unbound, tongue shrunk to a starling's.

Remember him leaning to bang his pipe on the hearth,
flickering in matchlight as he sat back
sucking the flame into a hot glow,
his magician's smoke billowing into the room.

She does not go there.
Nowadays we find her in the kitchen,
slicing the loaf, sliding the bread under the grill,
yoghurt spooned in dishes and a bowl of syrup
cooling on the sill.

Outside the house, the blinkered horse stands
like a ghost, with his cart,
stands like a ghost till his skin grows translucent
and his bones smoulder with phosphorus.

It's all still here:
the lights are on in number 36 and breakfast laid,
the milk poured, waiting.

Tapetum Lucidum

It pools blue light at spill-point
before an unexpected birch,
its scatter of leaves.

In dreams, he'd graze below this birch,
its slender branches reaching
to a windless sky.

Now the meadow scuds away,
its close-cropped grass drenched
in mist.

Without him, the sapling secures
its own horizon,
a knuckle of root sunk in the Earth
and that bruise of dark light above.

The structure is noted: blood vessels,
tapetum, retina.
There is the sound of metal instruments
being placed carefully in trays.

No one registers
the smallest shadow of a bird,
a confetti of fireflies orbiting the trunk,
the stray leaf drifting to the ground.

The eye is bagged, discarded.
Surfaces are sterilized.

In his own dark world,
the horse waits.

Rainer Maria Rilke

The Carillon, Bruges

Soft singing of the mad woman
behind the grille, a yellowed Christ
laid on a longship of candles.
Behind the dark tree of this altar
the nuns' whispers flit like bats
and against the warm dome of the abbey
the carillon falls, grey snow, lonely
as the slow surf at dusk in summer.
Lonely as windows behind which
no body has passed all winter, lonely
as the girl's glance behind the tram's glass,
lonely as velvet into which a ring is pressed,
and lime leaves settling on the canal
rightfully unaware of the coming amber.
Lonely as the swan, that slender saint
and inaudible atmospheres
still signalling from the flames.

Translated by Will Stone

Will Stone

The White Moor

Gripping nature's golden key
and breathing to a built in obeisance,
like pack mules we ascend the old road
where the fanatics cannot go,
the dread men of conviction,
for their acid burns nothing here,
their wild foreground gestures fade.

A celebration of some kind,
crowds line the lane, beech branches
atop the hard mud banks swept by the
gentle squall of new leaves and rain.
We are on our way to the white moor
where heather posies and yellow grasses
lap around the black bergs of ponies.

Loneliness loved and the little church
held nobly in the fold, the sudden punch
of a farm dog at the limit of a chain,
head rising out of the swell, gone again.
Foals circle the mother's barrel of blood,
turning, tracing, their huge dark eyes
a treasure whose origin is never located.

A solitary rider passes unnoticed
signalling to the shy opening of ferns.

Anne Lawrence Bradshaw

Different Skies

My sister and I have woven the sun,
drifting
on different horizons
where rain falls up, backwards in time
opposite ends
of the same sky.

I want to ask her:
do you remember how we burned
through those summer days,
the wheels on our bikes spinning with dusty heat,
the smell of tarry roads mingling with the salt-sweet air,
our sweat and playful fury?

Remember how we kept house
waiting for the new baby to arrive?
It was the summer when all the rain disappeared.
The blue of the sky a given
like the serried stand-pipes, guardians standing
on desiccated streets.
And, sister, a strange fragility
locked you to me.

At night, we felt the scorch begin to fade,
but instead of sleeping
we opened the bedroom window as wide as we dared.
We heard the garden's yearning, sucking drily
for water, rustling and greedy
for life.

We waved to boys as they walked home,
the moon rising above them.
Our thin cotton nightclothes brushed daringly
next to the window, next to our skin.
And somewhere in the darkness I know
you were thinking of our mother too,
threaded, spun out, on the long hem of time
waiting for the baby to come.

Sister, your red hair was like flames then.
It threatened to set fire
to the dry, yellow grass.
And in the morning, it would burn up our pillow,
ignite the sun, threaten
to leave it smoking in the places
where we'd leave our childhood dreams.

We are leaving now
my sister and I, wings outstretched
in different skies.

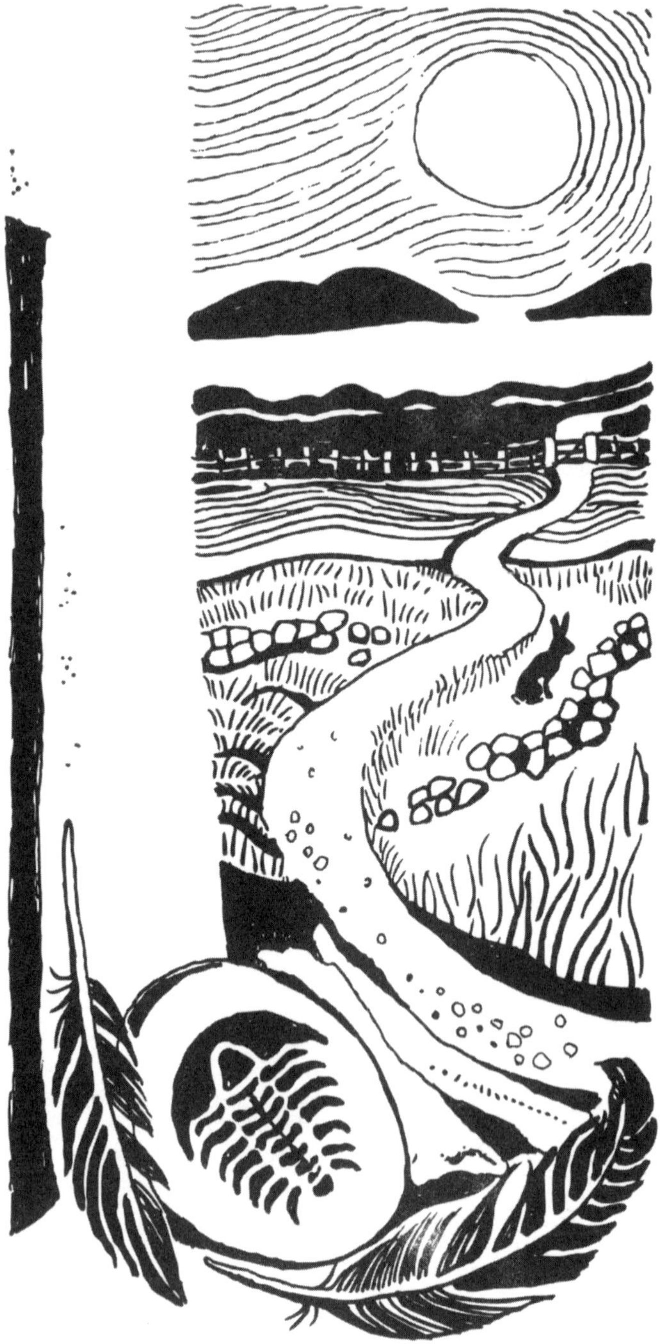

Josephine Balmer

A Sense of Marvel

Ocean Vuong: *Night Sky with Exit Wounds* (Cape Poetry, 2017)

Every now and again a writer bursts onto the literary world with a voice that is so individual, so of its own kind, yet at the same time so instantly recognisable, that it feels as if it has been in existence for ever. This year the debut collection by Ocean Vuong, *Night Sky with Exit Wounds*, has been heralded on both sides of the Atlantic as a major new work from a poet who will assuredly leave a lasting mark. Vuong's own extraordinary story, as a refugee who arrived in the US from Vietnam at the age of two, and who did not read proficiently until the age of eleven – the first member of his family to be literate – but has since been showered with poetry awards and honours, as well as being nominated as one of *Foreign Policy* magazine's 100 Leading Global Thinkers, all adds to the sense of marvel.

Given Vuong's intriguing backstory, the collection could have risked becoming biographically reductive. Yet there are several Oceans here: the refugee haunted by his homeland in 'Aubade With Burning City', deftly – and powerfully – juxtapositioning scenes of horror from the fall of Saigon with lines from Irving Berlin's 'White Christmas'. Or the street-smart New York City resident who in 'Notebook Fragments' records 'I'm gonna lose it when Whitney Houston dies'. He is both the confident lover of 'Thanksgiving 2006' ('I am ready to be every animal/you leave behind') and the hesitant boy exploring his gay sexuality in 'Because It's Summer' ('you say *thank you thank you thank you*'). In 'The Gift', he is the loving son teaching his mother the English abc as a strand of her black hair becomes the fourth letter, D, 'written /on her cheek'. In 'In Newport I Watch My Father Lay His Cheek to a Beached Dolphin's Wet Back', he is the son troubled by his father's violence and desertions ('I am chasing my father/the way the dead chase after/days'). Perhaps tellingly, in a 2016 interview with *The New Yorker*'s Daniel Wenger, Vuong revealed how his forename is, in itself, a construct (his birth name was Vinh Quoc), deriving from a conversation his mother had with a customer at the nail salon where she works. This weaving of poetic persona and lyric first person, playfully underscored in 'Someday I'll Love Ocean Vuong', reminds us how, in the most reflective poetry, the weaving of 'I' and 'you' is always complex, an intricate pattern of art and life.

The multiplicity of voices is echoed in the diversity of poetic forms

Vuong employs. The couplets of 'Self Portrait as Exit Wounds' and 'Homewrecker' give way to the free, discursive lines of poems such as 'Trojan' or 'Aubade With Burning City' and then the split lines of 'Of Thee I Sing'. These, in turn, disintegrate into the line-spaced prose of 'My Father Writes From Prison' ('there are things/I can only say in the dark') and then the full prose poem of 'Immigrant Haibun'. 'On Earth We're Briefly Gorgeous' mixes all forms in its various sections, from the prose narration of an encounter with a stranger ('He was divorced') to the heady, lush urgency of:

> Say surrender. Say alabaster. Switchblade.
> Honeysuckle. Goldenrod. Say autumn.
>   ('On Earth We're Briefly Gorgeous')

Most affecting of all is the 'Seventh Circle of Earth', based on a 2011 newspaper report detailing the murder of a gay couple 'by immolation in their home in Dallas, Texas'. Here the poem is a blank space, punctured by footnote numbers which lead to the lines themselves, buried beneath, a chilling, reduced font metatext to the silence above:

> 3. refuse me. / Our faces blackening / in the photographs along the
> wall. / Don't laugh. Just tell me the story / again, / of the sparrows
> who flew from falling Rome, / their blazed wings. / How ruin
> nested inside each thimble throat / & made it sing
>   ('Seventh Circle of Earth')

Such variety might stem from the poet's youthful exploration of his craft. Certainly there is a sense of exuberance throughout; 'Yikes' he writes (twice) in 'Notebook Fragments' while 'Ode to Masturbation', with its celebration of 'being human...the briefest form/of forever', speaks for itself.

Yet the reader is never left in any doubt of who 'Ocean Vuong' might be as a poet and as a poetic voice. In addition, his presence is so strong, as many reviewers have mentioned, that we are left wanting more. For instance, how did his family respond to his sexuality? Or to the way they are portrayed in the poems? In a conversation with Andrew McMillan, published in the Summer 2017 issue of *Poetry London*, Vuong explains how his family's illiteracy gives him a freedom from 'repercussion' to which many poets would not have access. Yet, at the same time, as he notes wistfully, the fact that they cannot read his books also means that they are excluded from that large and hugely significant part of his life.

Interestingly, a new prose poem, 'A Letter To My Mother That She Will Never Read', just published in *The New Yorker*, explores physical abuse by his mother during his childhood with gut-wrenching precision and honesty, detailing the bruises the poet would lie about to his teachers or the 'time you threw the box of Legos at my head. The hardwood dotted with blood.'

These incidents are not addressed directly in *Night Sky with Exit Wounds* where the poet's mother is a fierce but more benign figure: 'When they ask you/where you're from,' she reminds in 'Headfirst', 'tell them your name/was fleshed from the toothless mouth/of a war-woman'. Instead the collection, like its apparent anchor text, Homer's *Odyssey*, appears father-haunted, veined with the void of paternal absence, from the ghosted dedication 'to my mother [& father]' to the poem ironically named for his father's favourite Luther Vandross song 'Always & Forever'. As 'Someday I'll Love Ocean Vuong' reminds: 'Your father is only your father/until one of you forgets'. Similarly, in the dream-like sequence of 'Telemachus', the poet pulls his father's body out of the water:

> found
> the way a green bottle might appear
>
> at a boy's feet containing a year
> he has never touched.
> ('Someday I'll Love Ocean Vuong')

And in 'Odysseus Redux', the apparition returns:

> Back from the wind, he called to me
> with a mouthful of crickets –
>
> smoke & jasmine rising
> from his hair.
> ('Odysseus Redux')

Here the wild strangeness of the imagery, not to mention the otherness of the classical setting – especially for a writer whose engagement with western language started so late – all add memorably to the sense of another, recovered world shimmering through the mist. As 'To My Father / To My Future Son' urges of the written book:

> Use it to prove how the stars
>   were always what we knew
>
>   they were: the exit wounds
>   of every
>   misfired word.
>   ('To My Father / To My Future Son')

Whether writing of tangled family relationships or celebrating the healing metamorphoses of erotic love ('The way a field turns/its secrets/into peonies'), there is inventive, mesmerizing poetry, both playful and intensely personal. A poetry that hovers on the edge of meaning like consciousness at the moment of waking yet still remains accessible, inclusive. As 'Devotion' explains:

>   the way snow
> touches bare skin – & is,
>   suddenly, snow
> no longer.

Abegail Morley

Roy McFarlane: *Beginning with Your Last Breath* (Nine Arches Press, 2016)
Stephanie Conn: *The Woman on the Other Side* (Doire Press, 2016)

McFarlane's debut, *Beginning with Your Last Breath,* is a grounded collection, a man's journey through a life held by a love that knits itself deeper with each passing year; a love that is expelled with his first breath and continues after his mother's last, when she's 'hiding the knowing/ of her ending' ('Hiding'); a love that he passes to his own children, 'I cried when they had to cleave open the ripe/ melon womb to scoop out the heart of flesh and redness/ that was my second child.' ('I cried').

It is unsurprising then, given its central theme that McFarlane chooses as an epigraph to the first section a quote about a love that is whole, nourished, contained:

> The word for love, *habib*, is written from right
> to left, starting where we would end it
> and ending where we might begin.

It is a perfect choice for a collection that takes us on a cyclical journey of love – familial, platonic, sexual, spiritual interspersed by a hate (both political and racial) that etches its story leaving scars on skin. The lines, taken from 'A Soldier's Arabic' by the American poet Brian Turner, go on to tell of ending a war 'as an echo of history' and it is the echo of McFarlane's heritage that reverberates through these pages long after closing the book.

This sonorous collection is divided into distinct sections, each exploring aspects of the poet's life. It opens with the powerful poem 'Papers' where we meet the young poet just as his mother is showing him his adoption papers, when 'the smell of cornmeal porridge still coloured the air' and he is 'falling between the lines' until the tenderness of her voice draws him 'out of the margins'.

Here is a poet whose voice is never marginalised; it is sturdy and muscular in telling us how it feels to be part of a black family in 'The black corner of Wolverhamption', in Tipton, 'God's belly button/ of the Universe' ('Tipton'), of sporting heroes such as John Barnes 'the genius, the wizard that scored against Brazil' whose goal was disregarded by a plane 'filled with the England team and supporters,/ that goal don't count, the one scored by the nigger' (*'The Tebbit Test (Patriotism)*')'. He speaks candidly of racism, a friend 'pointing to the colour of his skin' saying, 'I'm tired of fighting and fitting in' ('Saturday Soup') of 'The Tebbit test, that litmus test of Britishness', of 'Blacks, Asians and Whites caught up in the winter of Maggie's policies' (Burning with a rage that Babylon would never understand…).

There is rage in this collection, a rallying against all that is wrong in the world, and a hunger for one where people 'listen with ears and not with their eyes' ('A Love Supreme'), but overwhelmingly there is love of family, humanity and poetry.

> If poetry could take the pain away
> it would begin with your last breath;
> capture it, re-write, re-verse your life.
> ('Beginning with Your Last Breath')

For me, it is the final verse of Brian Turner's poem that sums up McFarlane's collection, his approach and tenacity, his deft word choice and his quest for love to conquer hate:

> This is a language made of blood.
> It is made of sand, and time.
> To be spoken, it must be earned.

The Woman on the Other Side is the debut collection from a poet who comes with an impressive pedigree. Stephanie Conn won the inaugural Seamus Heaney Award for New Writing in 2015, having been shortlisted for the Patrick Kavanagh Prize the year before.

Published by Doire Press this is a wide-ranging collection – there are ekphrastic poems based on the works of Klimt, Hopper and Vermeer that rub shoulders with the personal, dealing with loss and internal conflict. The poems ring true throughout, whether she is in Tsvetaeva's Russia, having Christmas dinner in Canada or burrowed in the contours of a lavender field.

It is the themes of the opening poem that the poet comes back to time and again – feeling alien, alone, not only lost in countries, but at times in her own skin:

> Our bedroom has two doors. One leads to rooftops
> and a metre square of shade. It's where I go to focus
> on slate tiles tilting towards the sky.
> ('Maria Annastraatje, Leeuwarden')

Like the two doors in the room, Conn often has two responses to her environment – the physical and the emotional. However, a third dimension rises between the lines as Conn begins the exploration of self, a quest to find The Woman on the Other Side. As the poet takes on another person's story in 'Fair Trade', the life of a painter or sitter, she struggles to find her own story, reshape it and find her inner core.

> Forgive me. It is less my story to tell than yours, and yet
> having come to hear it spoken from your lips, I know
> it can travel great distances.
>
> ('Fair Trade')

> I do it slowly
>
> let them go one by one, making sure to unhinge
> the most stubborn stains and bruises
> that still reside in the frontal lobe
> searching out receptive transmitters.
>
> ('What We Pass On')

The poems in this collection are rewarding and unflinching. Conn lays herself bare in each with an honesty that is touching, poised and considered. She shows us the unsettling hard edges of life, how childhood and landscape transform us. Conn vividly brings each to life. Her language is both skilful and rich, each section reflects and builds on the previous to create a collection that bristles with life.

There are elements of a travelogue as Conn documents her memories of places she has visited, allowing the shackles of history to creep through her bones into ours, showing how over time a life can shift like tectonic plates. The poems take us on a journey that is both geographical and impassioned:

> Here nothing rots, the dead remain preserved forever dead
> between the barren hills and freezing desert nights.
> Yet further south, algae and lichen make the most
> of marine fog and perennials, and woody scrub
> suck on clouds entrapped by faulted mountains.
>
> And though the arid plains are littered with abandoned
> nitrate mining towns, the Peruvian song-sparrows sing
> and lemons will grow on the shores of the salt marshes
> while the villagers in Chungungo catch fog in mesh nets
> so moisture can condense and trickle into copper troughs.
>
> ('Absolute Desert')

Poems focus heavily on the external landscape, often parched, desolate or defeated:

> They say, at night, you can hear the wings of bats flap
> as they leave their box, hidden inside the stagnant sea
>
> and that the cross glows violently in the moonlight
> when they settle in the roped-off Wollemi Pine.
>
> ('Wurrungwuri')

Conn is a confiding tour guide and navigates an often-difficult terrain with an assured step, each poem speaking of endurance and survival. There are times when she is 'ready to be swallowed whole' when skin forgets 'how to heal as quickly as it did'. But despite this there is an overwhelming desire to persevere and see it through.

We travel from Tasmania to the Netherlands where the poet struggles with the language, the 'guttural place names all tongue and throat: / Groningen, Maastricht, Utrecht' whilst her partner was a natural and

> couldn't wait to track down a local
> to ask how to say I love you? *Ik hou van you,*
> – you said, content with your acquisition.
>
> ('Wie is de Vrouw on de Overkant?')

The Woman on the Other Side is a well-structured collection where neither the poet nor the poems wander. It is a voyage of discovery, a pilgrimage of childhood, where she pays homage to great artists and their sitters, whilst trying to rebuild a body touched by life's fractures.

CHOSEN BROADSHEET POET

Laura Potts is twenty years old and lives in West Yorkshire. She has twice been named a Foyle Young Poet of the Year and Young Writer. In 2013 she became an Arts Council Northern Voices poet and Lieder Poet at the University of Leeds. Her poems have appeared in *The Yorker*, *Now Then* and *The Looking Glass*. Having recently studied at The University of Cape Town and worked at The Dylan Thomas Birthplace in Swansea, Laura is now currently the Editor for Creativity at *The Yorker*.

Alma Mater

Widow-black and winter, evening took me south into
lamps burning blue in the dusk. Out and over my hometown musk
lay the hinterland hills breathing low in the dark. Still,
frostspark sharp on the city streets, holy rain sweet
in the winter and the wet, with no evening stars ahead I let
the pavement take me home. Through the town nocturnal, gloam

and grey, my chimney throat coughing its smoke, I saw aslope
on the city's slow spine those old black gates, the summer of my days
inside. Grief cracked my face. Those navy girls and me, a pace
always ahead. But in the pale stairwell light the ghost of my girlhood dead
in its fresh green spring and gone. From the roadside wet I looked on
at this child of light, her afterglow bright, her ashes of life

already black. The cold breath of loss on my face. At my back
a schoolbell cracked at the evening air. I saw Death at my table there
tipping his hat, and the years in my face that sank as I sat
at that desk at the back of the class. I remember that. And last,
on an old December evening, down hallways dark the wilting hymns
of girls turned ghosts before their time, I saw their eyes

like candles cold, like lights no longer leading home. Outside, to the bone
I shook and swung, the darkened seas that were my eyes done
and gone at the sight of myself. Each girl ringing her own passing bell.
Well, in that mist and half-dark morning, my face a clenching fist
in pavement pools, I saw that septic, terminal school
for what it was. No, I never went back, of course.

I tipped my compass north.

Swansea Son

He is here in my autumn of age
the riverlight through windowpanes,
the small-hour laughter,
the slim supple night,
and moonlight eyes on the history page.

I remember his name that giggled the stars
when the stage of the world lit its lights for him,
and I, summer's daughter,
he Swansea's son
whose words in the plash of the water
we hear in the echoes of hills. Still

the ghost in my arms in the cracked black night,
still in stairwells that old grey light that writes
of the deer shaping the dales, that writes
of bonfire-bright half-pint ale, that writes
of Death in His coat and tails:

you, man of words with the firefly eyes,
who didn't stay to see the wild spring flowers
riot on the mountainside, who died
like a steeple that cradles its bones,
and whose voice now sleeps beneath Wales' stones,

you, my lone man with the light, lord of all words,
whether I'm there with you or not, well, that's alright.

Ernie

It was then when the wicker-swing firefly-night
cracked the darkness of March, its last winter light
dropping soft in the pond. The trees at night
had wept long like newborns, and riversong
tolled like all summer's flutes to me in my dungarees,
hand-me-down, patch-me-up boots. But beyond

stretched the darkness, the distance, you,
and somewhere a church bell's slick copper tongue
always calling, calling
one more day to your evening,
one more day to your tomb.

From the blackcurrant glow of the living room,
I remember him too, years away in the giggling garden,
counting the stars. Far, the blue face of moon
dropped the years in his eyes. In the sighs of the wind
came his history in time: me in my lavender afternoons,
my shrill schoolbell laughter, his comrades' cries

on a broken frontline. His sweetheart died, and often I saw him
dance in the kitchen light, the ghost of her bright
in his eyes again, the northern star the same
as that in Gallipoli's mines. Sometimes he bagpiped
it down in the drive. And bundled me up whenever I cried. Aye,

they say he was bred on a wild rustic chant,
that he came from the mire of low in this land,
that he merited nothing, his forebears weren't grand,
but I still hear the pipes in the valleys.

Holly

In a suitcase your years at the lit bus stop.
Laughing loud and long, the top
of your lungs a screaming fox,
you had stopped to tell me you were gone.

Yesterday a word dark on your lips. Chips
I remember we split in the rain, a fizzing
last laugh in a childhood lane, smacking
our knees as the trees threw their bats.

Again as the streetlamps hung in their hats
I remembered we dreamed at the back
of a class a lost and dizzy tomorrow.
Remember that? Most of those stars left long ago.

Holly. The river has forgotten your name. No,
your broken light the same to me,
cracked black by the decades we did not see
from your garden gloam. That night as I walked

the last mile home a scrap of your laugh clung
to the wind and your bicycle bell, fifty years long,
thinned to a song I have heard since then, your afterglow
gone. Do you remember the thunder like a great Amen?

I looked on.

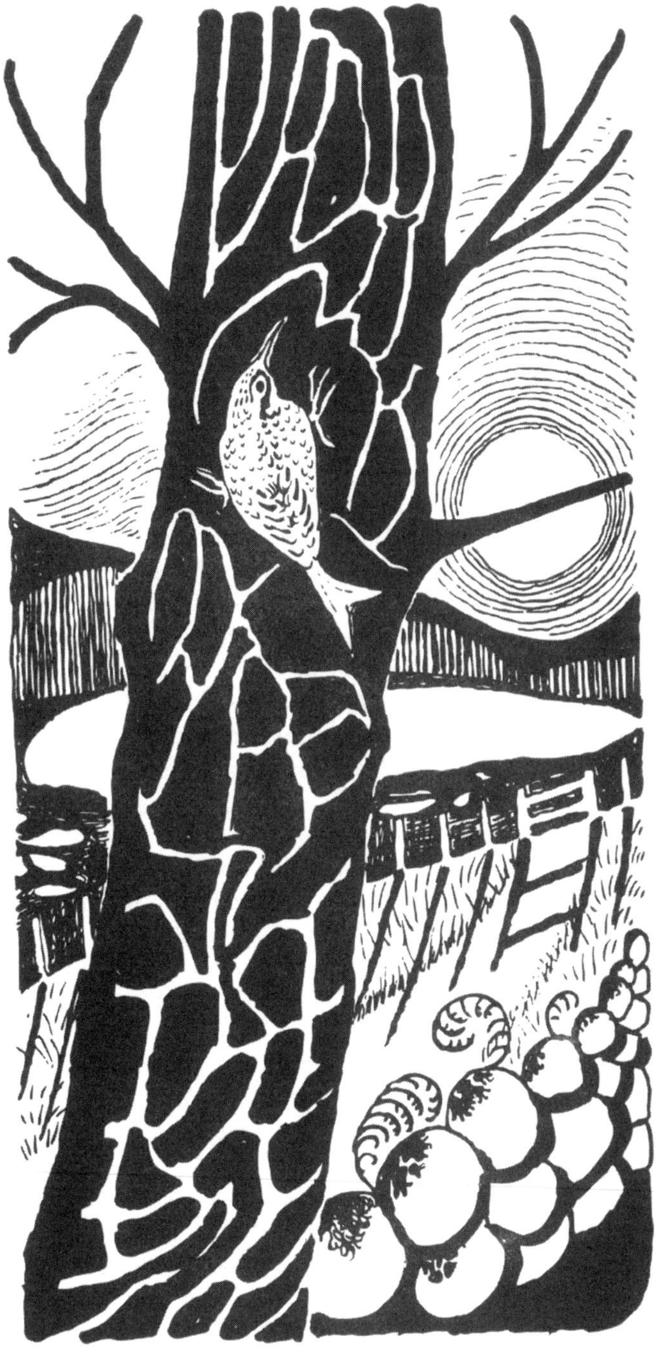

NOTES FOR BROADSHEET POETS

In his new collection (which he is sure, now, will be his last), *Injury Time* (Picador, 2017) – reviewed in this issue of *Agenda* by W S Milne) – Clive James appends a 'Letter to a Young Poet'. Most of us are familiar with Rilke's famous 'Letter to a Young Poet', excerpts from which appeared in the Reconsideration of Rilke issue of *Agenda* (Vol. 42 Nos3-4), and this Letter by Clive James, though different from Rilke's epistle, is as worth storing as the former.

Here I will, for the most part, take out the main points James makes, but you must remember he is so entertaining, so full of verve, and tongue-in-cheek in this 'Letter' that it is well worth reading the whole of the original text.

In his usual witty, amusing, articulate style, Clive James gives many sane punch-lines for the aspiring poet. He starts challengingly: 'First of all, give up if you can. Nobody who isn't neurotically driven should be in the game, because the chances of failure are too high, and the disappointments are too cruel'. He goes on to call 'stacking shelves' in a supermarket 'more useful to society than the average poem' and 'superior as a work of art'!

He warns the budding poet – who will only persevere if 'committed to a burning Miltonic compulsion' by destiny – not to be too sensitive about reactions to his/her poetry, not to care about praise, and to be hardened to 'indifference' and 'blame'. Important, also, not to be in a rush to publish but to wait until you are sure that the work is 'really finished' and you can even 'wonder how you did it'.

He also suggests keeping a notebook ('an ordinary quarto exercise book will do fine') and transferring the best bits to a 'work book', then ultimately to the computer. I would imagine most of you will use your mobile phones or iPads for even the earlier exercises and prompts. Nothing should go into the work book, he advises, 'except poems asking to be finished', and then you have to practise technique or form and find an appropriate shape and sound for them.

Inspiration is important, even if a poem takes decades in the making for 'Eventually the poem will tell you it is done by asking no more' when 'the whole thing sings' – or it 'will tell you it was misconceived by just lying there, saying nothing. Abandon it then'.

He suggests having a 'brilliant, sensitive, and critically scrupulous friend' to read your work on the condition 'only if his objections are those that you would have made yourself, given time'. The caveat is: 'if he objects to your basic individual tone, shoot him'!

He talks about the advantages and disadvantages of critics. Even hostile critics, who might have 'tin ears' with their 'brain-dead scorn', he says, are on your side 'if they quote you'. Critics who praise you are particularly dangerous, he states, and not worth depending upon as they might well change their minds the next time.

Listen to this:

> If you start thinking about your reputation, or even about your career as a poet, you are in the wrong frame of mind. What matters most is the poem, not the poet.

Regarding role models if you think you need one, it is vital, he urges, only to copy the 'sense of order' they bring to their phrases, not how they lived their often disorderly, dodgy lives, for 'the idea that only an intense life can produce intense poetry is a very bad one'.

He speaks of editors, too: 'the very best are usually poets themselves, so they have felt all this on the skin'; he adds, that even if an editor doesn't take to the poems you send in, always try again, as another poem may be accepted another time.

The editor, he says, 'is more concerned with printing something attractive to read than with helping to decide starting positions in the world-historical struggle towards immorality'!

Personally I would like to add here, that I, for one, am interested in printing something vital and musical, not simply something 'attractive' to read.

He does offer some reassurance: 'If even a few people remember a line or two in a poem you wrote, you're not just getting there, you're there. That's it: and all the greater glory is mere vanity', for 'nothing matters except your new poem' and 'your status as a poet is a side issue'.

He ends the letter as he began implying that if it turns out that you weren't, after all, born to be a poet, what you will be left with is your sense of dedication which you can put into doing something else – 'just as long as you get enough spare time to go on reading poetry, the second best thing to writing it, as I'm sure you would agree'.

A particularly memorable line from the poem 'Too Many Poets' in his new collection, *Injury Time*, is worth heeding and maybe should be inscribed at the top of every workbook:

> True poets should walk singing as they weep.

Patricia McCarthy

BIOGRAPHIES

Shanta Acharya is the author of eleven books. Her latest, *Imagine: New and Selected Poems*, is published by HarperCollins (India). www.shantaacharya.com

Jean Atkin's collection *Not Lost Since Last Time* is published by Oversteps Books and she has also published five poetry pamphlets and a children's novel. Her poems have won various prizes and recent work appears in *Magma*, *Envoi*, *The North*, *Earthlines* and *The Moth*. She has held many residencies in both England and Scotland, and works in education and community projects. www.jeanatkin.com @ wordsparks

David Ball lives in Besançon, birthplace of Victor Hugo, and has been published in a number of magazines in England and Ireland. He is also the translator of poems by François Migeot and Jacques Moulin.

Josephine Balmer's most recent collections are *The Paths of Survival* (Shearsman) and *Letting Go: Thirty Mourning Sonnets and two poems* (Agenda Editions), both published in 2017. Previous collections include *The Word for Sorrow* (Salt) and *Chasing Catullus: Poems, Translations and Transgressions* (Bloodaxe). She has also translated, Classical Women Poets and Sappho (all Bloodaxe). *Piecing Together the Fragments*, her study of classical translation and contemporary poetry, was published by OUP in 2013. She writes on poetry and translation for publications such as the *TLS*, *New Statesman* and *The Times*, for which she sets the daily Word Watch and weekly Literary Quiz.

William Bedford is an award-winning poet, short-story writer, children's novelist and novelist. In 2014, he was shortlisted for the *London Magazine* International Short Story Competition; won first prize in the Roundel Poetry Competition, and first prize in the *London Magazine* International Poetry Competition. His *Collecting Bottle Tops: Selected Poetry 1960-2008* was published in 2009, *The Fen Dancing* in 2014, *The Bread Horse* in 2015.

Byron Beynon's work has appeared in several publications including *Agenda*, *The Independent*, *London Magazine*, *Cyphers*, *Poetry Ireland Review*, *Planet*, *The Sante Fé Literary Review*, *The Yellow Nib* and the human rights anthology *In Protest* (University of London and Keats House Poets). He co-ordinated the Wales section of the anthology *Fifty Strong* (Heinemann). Collections include *The Echoing Coastline* (*Agenda* Editions), *Cuffs* (Rack Press) and *Nocturne In Blue* (Lapwing Publications, Belfast).

Anne Lawrence Bradshaw was born in Halifax, West Yorkshire, in 1963. Her work has appeared (or is forthcoming) in *Orbis, Acumen, Artemis*, as well as in many online literary magazines. Currently acting as Writer Liaison with *E&GJ Little Press*, she now lives in Northumberland and is married with three children.

Since 2008, **Iain Britton** has had five collections of poems published, mainly in the UK. Recently, poems have been published or are forthcoming in the *Poetry NZ Yearbook, Takahe, Brief* (NZ) *Meniscus, foam.e* (Aust) *Harvard Review, Mantis, POETRY* (US) *STAND, Stride Magazine, Clinic, The Literateur, M58, The Black Market Re-View, The Fortnightly Review, Long Poem Magazine, Poetry Wales, Agenda* and *The High Window* (UK). A collection of new poetry THE INTAGLIO POEMS will be published by *Hesterglock Press*, 2017 (UK).

Thomas Day teaches English at Eton College, where he also runs the Praed Society for poets and songwriters. He is the editor of the English Association journal *The Use of English*. He has published critical essays and reviews in *Essays in Criticism*, *The Cambridge Quarterly*, *The Warwick Review*, the *TLS* and others.

Craig Dobson worked in retail for twenty years before gaining an MA in Creative Writing from Bath Spa University. He has had poems published in *The London Magazine*, *The North*, *Stand*, *Orbis*, *Butcher's Dog*, *The Interpreter's House*, *Poetry Salzburg Review*, *The Frogmore Papers* and the University of Stockholm's *Two Thirds North* magazine. He has work forthcoming in *Under the Radar*.

Adam Feinstein is an acclaimed British author, poet, translator, Hispanist, journalist, film critic and autism researcher. His biography of the Nobel Prize-winning poet, *Pablo Neruda: A Passion for Life*, was first published by Bloomsbury in 2004 and reissued in an updated edition in 2013 (Harold Pinter called it 'a masterpiece'). His book of translations from Neruda's *Canto General*, with colour illustrations by the celebrated Brazilian artist, Ana Maria Pacheco, was published by Pratt Contemporary in 2013. He also wrote the introduction to the Folio Edition of Jorge Luis Borges' *Labyrinths*, which appeared in 2007. His own poems and his translations (of Neruda, Federico García Lorca, Mario Benedetti and others) have appeared in numerous magazines.

John Fuller is a poet, novelist, critic and editor ('A significant presence in British letters': *The Times*). His *Collected Poems* were published in 1996 by Chatto and Windus, and his latest volumes are *Gravel in my Shoe* (Chatto, 2015), *A Week in Bern* (Clutag, 2016) and *The Bone Flowers* (Chatto, 2016). His critical book *Who is Ozymandias? and other puzzles in poetry* appeared 2011. *Dream Hunter*, an opera written with the composer Nicola LeFanu, was produced in 2012, and LeFanu's *The Crimson Bird*, to a text by Fuller, premiered at the Barbican in 2017. He was a Tutor in English, and is now an Emeritus Fellow, of Magdalen College, Oxford.

Matt Howard lives in Norwich, where he works for the RSPB. Matt is also a steering group member of *New Networks for Nature*, an eco-organisation that asserts the central importance of landscape and nature in our cultural life. His debut pamphlet, *The Organ Box*, was published by Eyewear.

Rebecca Hurst is a doctoral student at the University of Manchester where she writes poetry and researches Soviet fairy tales. Her work has appeared in various magazines including *Aesthetica, Antiphon, The Wild Hunt, Magma Poetry*, and *The Next Review*. Her chamber opera *Isabella*, written with the composer Oliver Leith, premiered in London in 2015. Forthcoming work includes the libretto of a new opera, *After the Fall*, written in collaboration with Helgi Rafn Ingvarsson, which premieres in London in May 2017.

Mimi Khalvati has published eight collections with Carcanet Press, including *Child: New & Selected Poems*, a Poetry Book Society Special Commendation, and *The Meanest Flower*, shortlisted for the TS Eliot Prize. She has received a Cholmondeley Award, a major Arts Council Writer's Award and is a Fellow of the Royal Society of Literature. She is also the founder of The Poetry School. Her most recent collection, *The Weather Wheel* (Carcanet 2014), was a Poetry Book Society Recommendation and Book of the Year in *The Independent*.

Jane Lovell has had work published in a variety of anthologies and journals including *Earthlines, Poetry Wales, Mslexia, the North, Dark Mountain and Zoomorphic*. She won the Flambard Prize in 2015 and was recently shortlisted for the Basil Bunting Prize. Jane is currently working on her first collection for Agenda Editions.

W S Milne is a regular contributor to *Agenda*, and is a trustee of the magazine. He has just completed a play in Scots on Queen Margaret.

Jessica Mookherjee is a poet of Bengali origin. She grew up in Wales and now lives in Kent. She has been published in many print and online journals including *Agenda, Interpreter's House, The North, Rialto, Under the Radar* and *Antiphon*. Her pamphlet *The Swell* was published by TellTale Press in 2016. Her poems appear in various anthologies including *Templar 2016*, Eyewear's *Best of British and Irish Poets 2017* and Paper Swans' *Chronicles of Eve*. She won the Paragram Prize in 2016 for her poem 'The Beast'.

Abegail Morley's latest collection, *The Skin Diary*, is published by Nine Arches Press. Previous collections are published by Pindrop Press and her debut, *How to Pour Madness into a Teacup* (Cinnamon Press) was shortlisted for the Forward Prize Best First Collection. She blogs at The Poetry Shed.

Aileen Paterson lives in Northern Ireland, where she is currently studying Creative Writing.

Stuart Pickford is the recipient of an Eric Gregory Award. His first collection, *The Basics*, was published by Redbeck Press (2002) and shortlisted for the Forward Best First Collection Prize. His second collection is *Swimming with Jellyfish* just out from smith/doorstop. Stuart lives in Harrogate and teaches in a local comprehensive school.

James Roberts lives in the Black Mountains of Wales. Recent poetry has been published by *Agenda, Cinnamon* Press, *Little Toller* and *Corbel Stone Press*. He edits *Zoomorphic* magazine.

Tony Roberts' fourth book of poems, *Drawndark*, appeared in 2014. He is also the author of an essay collection, *The Taste in My Mind* (2015), and the editor of *Poetry in the Blood* (2014), all from Shoestring Press. Concerning Roberts' poetry, Al Alvarez wrote of 'an authentic adult voice, tender, ironic, relaxed and highly educated'. Reviewing his prose, John Forth found 'a detailed map of the age ... condensed to appear as table talk'.

Robyn Rowland lives in Ireland and Australia. She regularly works in Turkey. She has 9 books of poetry. Robyn's poetry appears in national and international journals, in 40 anthologies, and in 7 editions of *Best Australian Poems*. She has read in many countries e.g, Bosnia, Serbia, Austria, Turkey, Canada, India, and Portugal. Her two books in 2015 are *Line of Drift* from Doire Press, Ireland, and the bi-lingual *This Intimate War Gallipoli/Çanakkale 1915 – İçli Dışlı Bir Savaş: Gelibolu/Çanakkale 1915* published in Australia and in Turkey, with trans by Mehmet Ali Çelikel.

Omar Sabbagh is a widely published poet and critic. Two of his extant collections are: *My Only Ever Oedipal Complaint* and *The Square Root of Beirut* (Cinnamon Press, 2010/12); *To The Middle of Love*, his fourth collection, was published with Cinnamon Press in January 2017. His Beirut novella, *Via Negativa: A Parable of Exile* was published by Liquorice Fish Books in March 2016. A Dubai sequel to the latter, *From Bourbon to Scotch,* is forthcoming in early 2017. He has published essays on George Eliot, Ford Madox Ford, G.K. Chesterton, Robert Browning, Henry Miller, Lawrence Durrell, Joseph Conrad, and many others; as well as on many contemporary poets. His latest book is a collection of critical essays on literature, *Disciplined Subjects and Better Selves* (Anaphora, September 2016). He now teaches at the American University in Dubai (AUD).

David Seddon is from Liverpool and works as a counsellor in Congleton, Cheshire. Amongst other places, his poems have appeared in *The Interpreter's House, Poems in the Waiting Room, Antiphon, Ink Sweat and Tears, Poetry Scotland, Lighten Up* online and several anthologies including *Sculpted, Poetry of the North West*. He has had many landscape photographs printed in magazines. He has worked as a teacher, arts administrator, musician and for the Royal Navy. On Twitter he is Contented Counsellor: https://twitter.com/SeddonDavid.

Will Stone is a poet, essayist and literary translator. His first poetry collection *Glaciation* (Salt, 2007), won the international Glen Dimplex Award for poetry in 2008. A second collection *Drawing in Ash* appeared from Salt in May 2011. Shearsman Books republished these in 2015 and published a third collection *The Sleepwalkers* in April 2016. Arc Publications published his translations of the poetry of Georg Trakl (2005), Emile Verhaeren (2013) and Georges Rodenbach (2017). Seagull Books will publish his *Collected Poems* of Georg Trakl in 2018.

Seán Street's latest collection is *Camera Obscura* (Rockingham Press, 2016.) Prose includes *The Poetry of Radio* (Routledge,2013),*The Memory of Sound* (Routledge, 2015), and *Sound Poetics: Interaction and Personal Identity,* (Palgrave, 2017). Among works are books on Gerard Manley Hopkins and the Dymock Poets. He is Emeritus Professor at Bournemouth University and lives in Liverpool.

John Wheway's work has been published previously in *New Measure, Stand, Magma, The Warwick Review, Poetry Review,* the *Yellow Nib, Poetry Quarterly,* the *Compass Magazine,* three Templar anthologies and *The Echoing Gallery* from Redcliffe Press. His chapbook *The Green Table of Infinity* appeared from Anvil, and Faber and Faber published his novella *Poborden*. He has a Creative Writing MA from Bath Spa University.

Lawrence Wilson grew up near Chicago, Illinois and has degrees in drama, education and interdisciplinary art. He has sung and acted professionally and has exhibited his pottery, sculpture, installations and artist's books in the UK and the USA and online. His fiction, poetry, essays and reviews have appeared in *Agenda, Albedo One,* Paper Swans Press (*The Best of British, The Poetry of Roses, The Darker Side of Love), Poet's Cove, Art and Academe, Prairie Light Review, The Art of Monhegan Island,* and on Salon.com and Monhegan.com. His first collection, *The April Poems,* was published in 2016 and his second lot of *April Poems* in 2017.

Lynne Wycherley lives on a headland in the West Country. Fond of the Romantic tradition but also alert to science, she currently combines poetry with health research and is a contributor to *The Ecologist.* Her *Listening to Light: New & Selected Poems* was published by Shoestring Press in 2014.